Library
Building
Projects

Library Building Projects

Tips for Survival

SUSAN B. HAGLOCH

1994
Libraries Unlimited, Inc.
Englewood, Colorado

LIBRARIES UNLIMITED, INC.
P.O. Box 6633
Englewood, CO 80155-6633
1-800-237-6124

Library of Congress Cataloging-in-Publication Data

Hagloch, Susan B.
   Library building projects : tips for survival / Susan B.
Hagloch.
   xiii, 151 p. 17x25 cm.
   Includes bibliographical references and index.
   ISBN 0-87287-980-1
   1. Library buildings--United States--Design and
construction. I. Title.
Z679.2.U54H34 1994
727'.8--dc20   93-43927
                                                    CIP

Contents

Acknowledgments

I would like to thank all of the colleagues and friends whose support helped me to survive my building project and whose ideas have contributed to this book: Cathi Alloway, Julie Brooks, Jim Bouchard, Mary Ann Culbertson, Luren Dickinson, Laurie Drapp, Cheryl Foote, Alan Hall, Pat Hillmer, Linda Hren, Camille Leslie, Jim McPeak, Ann Miller, Rick Rubin, Susan Vermilya, and Lisa Wolfe.

Thanks go also to the anonymous tipsters with whom I shared busses and cafeteria tables at ALA and PLA conferences.

Special thanks to Curt Smock, AIA, of Koster & Associates, Architects for his rendering of the new Tuscarawas County Public Library shown on the front cover, and, of course, for steering us through the project start to finish.

Thanks to Mitchell's Studios, photographers in New Philadelphia, Ohio.

My deepest thanks to the staff of the Tuscarawas County Public Library who performed heroically throughout our project. Special thanks go to department heads Damaris Eisinger, Barbara Gildersleeve, Deborah McWreath, Wendy Mady, and Debra Tristano, who coordinated their various departments with the aplomb of seasoned generals.

And, of course, special thanks to my husband, Joe!

Introduction

Library building projects are usually once-in-a-lifetime events for the librarians in charge, being completely different from anything they usually do. Most librarians, in fact, go through their entire professional careers without having to manage such a project. Usually, by the time they realize they are going to be involved with one, the process is already underway, and they have had no time to pore over the literature on the subject to educate themselves, and to figure out what they need to know and where to learn it. Most of them simply blunder along, taking advice wherever they can find it. When at last the project is over, the librarians have learned many lessons, some of them painful. And they have thought many times, "Why didn't someone tell me x?"

This book is a collection of tips, warnings, and hints compiled during the course of one such project. The project in question was typical: The expansion and renovation of a main library building that was built in 1936 in a medium-sized town in a medium-sized U.S. state. The librarian—me—was a medium-sized, middle-aged woman with pretty good sense but no previous experience in the construction of anything more complicated than a birdhouse. As the project progressed I made the usual discoveries of things that I ought to have done at an earlier stage; things to keep an eye on; and ways to preserve my sanity, as well as that of my staff and patrons.

This book is divided, as such a project often is, into the various phases involved. The actual construction of the building is only one part of the whole experience. The first step is figuring out exactly what you want to do and learning if it is possible. Then you have to figure out how you are going to pay for the building. Most libraries, including mine, finance the building with a bond issue, so I have included a chapter on the lessons learned from a first defeat and the subsequent victory.

Preparing for construction is the next step. Before the construction trailers arrive, there are many things the library staff can do that will make ensuing events less traumatic. This is the time to prepare your staff, your public, and your building for the trials to come. During the construction, little can be done to alleviate the noise, the dust, and the everyday crises that develop. But there are ways to make these inconveniences more bearable.

Finally comes the worst part of all: the gala reopening, complete with refreshments, speeches by dignitaries, and last-minute glitches. But this too shall pass, and you will finally get back to running a library (if you still remember how).

This is not a project manager's manual. My experience with my building project didn't teach me everything to watch out for. Much that could have gone wrong didn't! We had no strikes or major accidents. The architect and general contractor were both professionals, good and true, which is not always the case. There were many problems that we didn't encounter and those I do not address in this book. In general, we had a lucky project. One outward sign of our good fortune was the fact that two weddings resulted from our activities. The architect married the interior designer, and one of the workmen married our processing clerk.

I firmly believe that we created a lot of the luck ourselves. We planned as much as could be planned, and we rolled with the punches when they came. It was standard procedure that the roofer removed all of the old flat roof one day, leaving only a tarp to cover the concrete ceiling below until the next morning. It was bad luck that it happened to rain that night. But it was good planning that we had miles of plastic sheeting on hand. And it was good sense that we gave our soaked staff the afternoon off after a morning of mopping and bailing.

My project was unique. Nevertheless, I believe, based on conversations with others who have had the same experiences, that it was fairly representative. Each project is different, but many related experiences are universal. This book will, I trust, make them plain.

"A Metaphysical Vision into the Future of Funding for Physical Facilities"

JOE NATALE

Consultant, Library Construction, Illinois State Library

(From *Illinois Libraries*, January 1990. Copyright 1990 by ALA. Reprinted with permission.)

"A satire is, of course, no poem."

—Edgar Allan Poe

*Once upon a midday merry
While I filed neat and cheery
Some construction field reports
Suddenly someone came banging
Like a hammer banging, banging
On my office door.
"This better be important," I muttered
"Or I'll be sore."*

*Presently my stress grew stronger,
Hesitating then no longer
"Sir," I said, "Or Ms.,
Your patience I implore
But I was working
When you came banging, banging
On my office door.
State your business, nothing more."*

*Open here I flung the door wide
When with a clumsy, awkward glide
Waddled in a granite Gargoyle
Of antique days of yore.
Then perched while tottering
As if teeter tottering
Just above my office door
Read on, there's even more.*

(Poem continues on page xii.)

The ghastly, grim beast wore a frown
On a face by rain worn down
The hoary visage was not gay
With wrinkled lips
Of cold command sneering
Perched and sneering, sneering
Just above my office door
Teetering as precariously as before.

Then, methought, the air grew dense
From the clumsy menace
As I sat engaged in guessing
Why the crooked sneer was burning
Like a fire burning, burning
Into my bureaucratic soul
I asked: "Is it a grant you came for?"
Quoth the Gargoyle, "There's no more!"

"Prophet!" I said, "Or Pest. O, horror,
Horror in what you said.
Yet I've had premonitions of doom
In the library construction boom.
Still I'll never cease hoping
With fervor hoping, hoping
For even more."
Quoth the Gargoyle, "Not any more."

But the Gargoyle thought me frantic
Pleading for more schematics
Of grand staircases, atriums and parapets
And piles of dark forest green carpets
Intensely I was begging
To the beast begging, begging
Just above my office door:
"Let's build some more!?!"

The Gargoyle considered me too bold
In staccato voice began to scold:
"You always sensed the program's fate
There's other demands upon the state
Don't count on funding
Endless funding, funding."
I tried: "Let's build some more!?!"
Croaked the Gargoyle, "You're such a bore."

Then my hopes began to glimmer
Blood pressure ceased to simmer
Spying the Gargoyle teetering
As if sea sick, teetering, teetering
Just above my office door.
Then with a thundering crash
Shattered on my office floor
Dashed to pieces and nothing more.

May these public works continue
Remodeling and building anew
With or sans construction grants
With elevators rising
Like columns rising, rising
Beyond the first floor
Accessible to the handicapped
And to many more.

1

In the Beginning ...

 Develop a long-range plan for your library, using the skills of trustees and community leaders. Solicit input from users and staff.

You can't sell a building project unless you know what it's for. It isn't enough to look around your library and say, "Boy, look how crowded those shelves are. We need more space." Or, "It sure would be nice to have a meeting room so I could have my Administrator's Support Group meet here, instead of driving across the state every three months." Your trustees and public have to be convinced of the need for new construction, or the project will never happen.

A long-range plan focuses on the specifics of what your library does, how it does them, and what it needs to do them better. Survey your public to find out what they want from you. (You may be surprised.) Survey your staff to find out what they perceive the library's needs to be. Discuss the issue with your board. The more people who are involved from the beginning, the more community support you will have.

Hire consultants to analyze your needs.

A feasibility study is vital. It will tell you whether what you want to do is possible. With its fresh viewpoint, it will also make suggestions that your staff and public haven't thought of. It will study your patterns of usage over the past ten years or so and project those patterns into the future, and it will take your needs and turn them into a workable plan.

Such studies are done by library consultants, by architectural firms, and by building consultants. Be sure to get someone who is familiar with both construction and library services. Libraries have unique functions and cannot easily be adapted to fit office- or school-like spaces. Some architectural firms specialize in library projects; these will have the best combination of expertise for you.

🏛 *Tour libraries that various architects have created, and talk to people who were there when the libraries were built.*

Choosing an architect is very ticklish. You must have an architect with library experience. However, some boards feel that they have to hire a local architect, even if the firm has no such experience. Invariably, the building doesn't work, so the board is unhappy, the staff is miserable, the public feels it didn't get its money's worth, and the architect's reputation takes a nosedive. Nobody needs this.

Your best means of finding an architect is to tour libraries that have recently been built or redone. Talk to the head librarian and the staff. What did they like about the architect? What did they dislike? Did the architect listen to staff concerns? Did the firm handle problems well and quickly? How does the library feel to you, the visitor? Take pictures or a videotape and report to your board. If possible, take the members on a field trip to a library you like that was designed by an architect you want to hire.

🏛 *Analyze your library's funding for the past ten years, with projections for the next ten. Can you afford not only to build but also to staff and supply the new space?*

Library funding is never carved in stone. Projecting the future is nearly impossible, but it has to be attempted. Even if you can get a bond issue or a grant to build, you still have the new space to support afterward. Your utility bills will change, because you will be heating and lighting a larger space. However, a new HVAC (heating, ventilating, and air conditioning) system will probably be more efficient and may save you money. You will need to consult with experts to get at least a ballpark estimate.

You will probably need new staff to cover the expanded space and to handle the expected increases in usage. Can you afford to pay them? How many new computers will you need? Adding machines? Staplers? It sounds trivial, but your supplies budget will be shot during the first month you're open if you don't plan ahead. Every new workstation will need to be furnished with these basic tools, and their costs can mount up fast.

🏛 *Explore grant possibilities.*

LSCA funds aren't the only ones available to help with library construction. Local industries often may be affiliated with foundations that will help finance community improvements. Libraries are a highly visible community resource and a good showcase for these foundations. A memorial fund is another possible source of funding. Some communities have established foundations in memory of a prominent citizen. Also, local service clubs may be willing to help. They usually have regular fund-raising projects and may be willing to donate this year's receipts to your project.

🏛 *Plan to fund at least 10 percent more than your architect estimates.*

The architect's estimate will include a contingency fund of about 10 percent of the cost, but you will need more. After construction begins, someone will think of something vital that got left out of the plans, or the contractor will suggest extras here and there that will improve something's function or appearance. You want to be able to say "Yes" to these things. A project like this is a once-in-a-lifetime thing, and you want it done right. And if, by some miracle, you don't use the extra money during construction, it will be available for post-occupancy changes, the purchase of adjacent property to expand your parking, or additional terminals or microfilm readers.

For a slightly more nightmarish vision of project funding, see "A Metaphysical Vision into the Future of Funding for Physical Facilities" in the introduction. (Apologies to Edgar Allan Poe.)

Planning a Library in One Week

EDWARD H. HEALEY

(From *American Libraries*, April 1991. Copyright 1991 by ALA. Reprinted with permission.)

Ever heard of a charrette? Superior, Wisc.; Winona, Minn.; and Waterloo, Newton, Dewitt, and Cedar Rapids, Iowa; have all had charrettes for the purpose of designing new libraries.

Take Superior, for example. To design its new public library, the city sought an architectural firm with special expertise in library design and selected my firm, Brown Healey Stone Sauer, located 400 miles away in Cedar Rapids. Superior's timetable called for the start of construction nine months after signing our contract. The obvious solution for their new "baby" was one we had used on many previous projects—a charrette.

"Charrette" is a French word meaning "cart." It came into use in architectural parlance in the early 1900s at the Ecole des Beaux-Arts in Paris. Studio projects were assigned to students, with a deadline for completing the project and turning it in, usually in 12 to 24 hours. Often these projects were due at midnight. Students traditionally worked feverishly, right up to the last minute, when a cart was wheeled down the aisles between the drafting tables. Their drawings were hastily placed in the cart—sometimes with a student or two riding the cart down the aisles putting the final touches on a drawing.

I came to know the charrette while a student at the Fontainebleau School of Fine Art in France and immediately saw its application in the Superior Public Library project. A charrette would allow us to get as many people as possible vitally involved in the design; it would allow us to maintain a very tight design schedule; and it would allow us to provide close personal attention at a crucial phase of the project—even though our office was 400 miles from the site.

Burning the Midnight Oil

A team of architects from Brown Healey spent the greater part of a week living—and working day and night—in Superior during April 1990. Additionally, a landscape architect, an electrical (lighting) engineer, a mechanical (heating, ventilating, air conditioning) engineer, a cost-control expert, a model maker, and a secretary/typist hired locally spent varying amounts of time working with us as part of the charrette team. The goal was to complete and obtain official approval of the schematic design, the first phase of the architectural work, at the end of one week.

Don't misunderstand: A great deal of work and decision making by many people was complete before the charrette began. The city had made the decision to abandon the rundown 1902 library building, which was in very bad condition. A building statement had been prepared by the library's director and staff and had been reviewed by library consultant David Smith.

The architects had already been retained to study three possible sites for the new library. One was a beautiful, historic, finely carved limestone post office building. Another was a generic site for a totally new building. The third was a supermarket building.

Although the fine, old post office was very tempting to everyone, thorough consideration of library staffing and costs for a multi-level building and the added costs of proper historic preservation and restoration clearly indicated the super-market was the best solution for the best price. Primary reasons for this were its excellent location on the best corner in downtown Superior, the large bay spacing, high ceilings, the structure's substantial construction quality, and the existing large, lighted parking lot on the site.

Before the charrette began, the architects prepared base plans of the site, researched applicable codes, and studied (along with the structural, mechanical, and electrical engineers) the selected building and site. The city invited people to participate, and a meeting schedule was arranged and distributed. A large room with suitable tables and display wall space was readied.

The charrette started on Sunday afternoon with a meeting with the library director followed by a tour of the old library and the supermarket. On Monday, an informational meeting open to anyone who wished to know what we were going to be doing that week was held in the library. Following the initial meeting, the architects met separately with representatives of the mayor's office, common council, library staff and director, library board, library building committee, local economic development corporation, city planning commission, building improve-ment district, public access cable television, city department of public works, planning and development department, and the mayor's commission for the disabled.

Each group was asked for its particular concerns and was invited to come back at any time during the charrette to see how we had dealt with their input. Minutes were kept of each of these meetings and made part of our final report. Late each afternoon and well into the night, the architects worked, designing and sketching.

Every morning during the charrette, the director, key library staff members, and the building committee met with the architects, who presented their work of the day and night before. The chief representatives were all encouraged to criticize and provide additional input. Each day the work evolved further and further toward the final schematic design.

The charrette room was open to the public throughout the week and people were encouraged to come in. One library staff member was a real regular, coming in to watch us work or to look over some of the myriad sketches that filled every inch of wall space.

The last day of the charrette was devoted largely to final preparations of the planning materials, which were assembled and printed in a 48-page brochure. Included in the presentation were floor plans, elevations, site plans, furniture layouts, spatial relationship matrix, cost estimate, and notes and minutes of meetings. Thirty copies were provided for the owner. Final presentation was made late that afternoon to the general public, the common council, and library trustees, followed by an official meeting of the trustees for approval of the schematic design phase.

A PR Bonus

Every charrette is different. Much of this, of course, is due to the mix of people involved in the process. One of our library charrettes was held in a vacant downtown store, where many people dropped by while shopping or on their lunch hours to provide ideas and suggestions. The public finds this a particularly exciting, dynamic process, which is good for public relations. Charrettes appeal to the media, too; they find them to be something they can show visually. Participants come away from the process supporting the project and able to explain the design to others.

Superior Library Director Paul Gaboriault, summed it up this way: "It was a great experience. Everyone got caught up in the excitement and enthusiasm of the charrette. When they realized that their ideas were being considered and they were being listened to, they were anxious to come back the next morning to see what new developments had taken place overnight."

During 36 years as an architect, Edward H. Healey has become a library specialist. The president of Brown Healey Stone Sauer, Cedar Rapids, Iowa, ALA-member Healey also serves on the Iowa State Library Commission.

Library Design: The Next Generation

MARTY MILLER

(From *Ohio Libraries*, September/October 1990. Copyright 1990 by Ohio Library Association. Reprinted courtesy of Ohio Library Association.)

The next generation of libraries may be characterized by their high tech design and machine oriented aesthetics, or they may have a more conservative, even ecclesiastical look and feel about them. This is based on a small sample of the range of designs produced by a group of architecture students at The Ohio State University.

Students in Architectural Design 343 designed the libraries based on location and usage requirements of the Karl Road Branch of the Columbus Metropolitan Library. Moody/Nolan, Ltd. designed the total library project which included the interiors with specialized shelving and furnishings, the site plan and the widening of Karl Road. The 20,000 square foot interior maximizes natural light, which, combined with a soft color palette, fashions a cool oasis that encourages browsing.

The students were required to visit a recently completed branch to gain insight into the way programmatic conditions are given form. The course, taught by Professor Robert Samuelson and Associate Professor Yousef Marzecki, is designed to put the students in a professional setting with specific, controlled objectives. Assisting the students in Marzecki's class during the two-quarter program were Amalia Iglesias, R.A., and Kay Onwukwe, designers with Moody/Nolan, Ltd. They reviewed the progress of the students' work and offered professional advice on control factors such as parking, circulation and shelving, as well as helping students with the functional aspects of their designs.

Students report that they gained an understanding about the importance of how a design must fit in with the surrounding neighborhood and they learned that public perception of the design and who will be using the facility are essential considerations.

This course is based on an actual program developed by the Columbus Metropolitan Library and presented to architects engaged to design branch libraries. The basic building and service program requirements included:

- A 7,500 square foot library facility

- Signage visible from main transportation arteries

- Specified number of parking places, including spaces for the handicapped, bicycles and motorcycles

- Convenient access for delivery vehicles and library users

- Appropriate landscape to screen the library from traffic noise and provide a transition from the parking area to the building entrance

Other requirements included appropriate shelving, sound controls, natural light controls, interior signage, use of sound-absorbing building materials, seating, display areas, security features and specifications for various service areas.

As an added bonus, all design proposals submitted by the students were entered in the Ohio Masonry Council Competition. Winners will be announced later this year.

Marty Miller is the owner of Miller Communications, which handles publicity for Moody/Nolan, Ltd.

2

The Bond Issue Campaign

🏛 *Find a campaign chair who carries clout in the community, preferably a local business leader who buys a lot of local media advertising.*

The library is usually not considered by the local media to be a hot news story. While library bond issues are terribly exciting to librarians, they are usually small compared to school issues, and editors may feel that there's nothing much to write about. Librarians don't usually have much influence on editors, but the community's big business leaders do. If your campaign chair is J. Getty Gotrocks, owner of Gotrocks Department Store, which buys a lot of advertising in the local paper, you can be sure that the city editor will be very interested in your campaign.

Library touts bargain levy

JOE MIZER

(From *The Times-Reporter*, 4-13-89, A-1, Dover-New Philadelphia, Ohio.)

Tuscarawas County Library officials have launched a vigorous campaign to pass a 0.3-mill bond issue which would pay for a major expansion and renovation project at the main library building in New Philadelphia.

The issue, designed to raise $1.5 million over 20 years, was rejected last fall by a narrow margin. But library officials are confident that a change in design will meet with voter approval in the May 2 primary.

"We got feedback from the public that they didn't like the look presented in the sketch last fall," said head librarian Susan Hagloch. "So we went back to the architect, and he came up with a much better match."

Hagloch noted that the new design compliments and maintains the library's historic architectural design and said the proposed 9,000-square-foot, two-story addition at the rear will be a perfect match. "You can't tell where the old stops and the new begins," she added.

It also incorporates all of the previously planned improvements, including the following:

- An elevator to provide total accessibility for the physically disabled.

- A meeting room for groups of up to 50 persons.

- A story hour room for children's programming.

- Increased space for library users, including quiet study areas.

- More space for books and other loan materials.

- Office and storage space for processing books.

- New bookmobile garage.

- New roof to eliminate leakage problems which have caused considerable damage to the interior.

The total project is estimated at $2 million, with the additional $500,000 to be provided from the board's building fund and fundraising events.

The bond issue, if approved, would cost the average homeowner (of real estate with a market value of $50,000) an additional $5.25 annually.

Opinion

The Reporter
Times
Founded July 10, 1903, Dover-New Philadelphia, Ohio

Jack D. Shores, President

Mark E. Raymond
Publisher

James E. Davis
Editor

Richard J. Farrell
Managing Editor

Sandra Stewart
Assistant Managing Editor

Paul Koloski
Editorial Page Editor

Page A-4; Wednesday, April 26, 1989

Say yes to the library

The Times-Reporter strongly urges voters participating in next Tuesday's primary election to support the 0.3-mill bond issue for expansion and renovation of the Neew Philadelphia library.

As the main repository of books and primary source of informational services in the five-unit county library system, the building at Fair and N. Broadway draws substantial traffic. Unfortunately, this has brought crowded conditions which won't be eased until more room is made available. The bond issue would raise $1.5 million over 20 years to expand the library by 9,000-square feet in an architectural style consistent with the present structure.

Besides overcrowding, other problems that would be alleviated by the inflow of bond issue funds are:

☐ The library's inaccessibility to handicapped countians, for whom an elevator would be installed;

☐ Lack of shelf space for books;

☐ Limited room for civic groups and reading classes to meet;

☐ A porous roof that has allowed damaging leaks to destroy library property. It will be replaced.

The total to be raised is a lot of money, but, spread among property owners in the expansive library district, it would amount to only an extra $5.25 a year for the owner of $50,000 property.

Considering that more than 16,000 area readers use the library, kicking in an extra $5.25—less than 1-1/2 cents a day—strikes us as a great bargain.

Its campaign materials this spring include a non-negotiable check to citizens stating the library in 1988 provided $10.3 million worth of services at an actual cost of $715,000. That translates to $14.38 worth of services for every dollar expended.

Hagloch says she is proud that in 1988 the library loaned 442,469 books which saved borrowers $8.8 million, and 15,970 videocassettes which saved them $319,400. And last year, the reference department also provided answers to 30,759 questions while librarians presented story hours to 3,660 children.

The library also loans records, audio cassettes, 16mm films, filmstrips, compact discs, framed art prints, projectors and computer software programs.

The main library building, located at 121 Fair Ave., NW was built in 1936 with a designed capacity to house up to 48,000 books and 100 periodical subscriptions. Today, it holds 73,000 books and 231 periodical subscriptions.

In 1936, there were 6,658 registered borrowers at the main library. Now it serves 16,541, not counting those who use library cards from other libraries.

It also serves as a processing center for the county bookmobile and for its branch libraries in Bolivar, Strasburg, Sugarcreek, and Tuscarawas.

The library district—those eligible to vote on the bond issue—includes voters in all areas of the county except Dover (which has its own library), Oxford and Clay townships, the west half of Salem, northern Mill and southern Union townships.

It is true that newspapers and other media follow very strict rules about covering political campaigns. Only news stories, editorials, and paid advertising are allowed. But a news story can say "The library is asking for a .5 mill levy to fund a building renovation and expansion" and bury the story in section Z, or it can wax lyrical about all of the projected improvements and be smack on the front page with a color photo. It all depends on the interest level of the editor.

🏛 *Plan a lot of special events that don't specifically relate to the campaign for the weeks immediately preceding the election.*

An interested editor will be more inclined to print stories about the library's observation of National Library Week or Banned Book Week, or a read-a-thon, or a special program, or a knockout display. Even if you can't mention the election, in order to conform to the rules governing the media and campaigning, this is a good way to keep your name in front of the public.

Hire competent bond counsel before you begin the process of filing for the election.

This comes under the heading of "simple common sense," which may not be so simple if you've never been involved in an election before. "How tough could it be?" you think. And you find out.

Because libraries come under a variety of governmental identities, you may find that your filing must go through the county commissioners or the city council, even if they have nothing whatsoever to do with the operation of your library. You will probably need official statements from local auditors or tax officers. The phrasing of these statements may be very particular, and what suits other entities may not be right for a library.

Every locale has its own system, and picking your way through the maze requires expert guidance. Do-it-yourself work can have disastrous results. A small town put a bond issue on the ballot for a new fire truck. It was a hotly contested issue, and it passed by a whisker. After they bought the truck, they discovered that they had made a tiny error in filing. The whole election was thrown out, and they had to give the money back!

Ask sympathetic organizations to endorse your issue publicly—the more publicly, the better.

Who are the people in your community who will benefit from your building project? If the building is to be made more handicapped accessible, it is the disabled. If you are gaining a new meeting room, it is the club and civic groups. If you will be expanding children's services, it is parents and caregivers. All these people can help you win voters, but you must seek them out and make them want to help. These people can create their own news stories in support of your cause. In our case, the local Handicapped Society picketed us, in the pouring rain, carrying signs that read IT'S OUR LIBRARY TOO—VOTE YES FOR ISSUE 1, and LET US IN—VOTE YES FOR ISSUE 1. This was very eye-catching and made the front page of the paper four days before the election.

Handicapped pickets point out need for levy

No access at county library for disabled

(From *The Times-Reporter*, Wednesday, April 26, 1989, A-3, Dover-New Philadelphia, Ohio.)

A handful of wet pickets stood and sat through the rain Tuesday morning outside the Tuscarawas County Public Library at New Philadelphia to push for passage of the library's 0.3-mill bond issue in the May 2 primary.

The pickets, many of whom were wheelchair-bound, are members of the county's Handicapped Society, and society director Dale Short said his crew planned to stay just an hour or so because of the rainy conditions.

"It's hard to get a lot of these people out," said Short, who was forced to watch from his car.

According to Short, the picketing was just the group's way of letting the public know how they feel about the levy.

The issue, designed to raise $1.5 million over 20 years, would pay for a major expansion at the facility and make the building accessible to the disabled.

"That's (passage of the levy) the only way you're going to get a wheelchair in there," Short said.

"We're tired of always looking in from the outside," said Arthur Souza, a society member on the picket line.

"We want people to notice us for a change," Souza said.

Money from the levy will be used to provide an elevator inside the building; a meeting room for public use; a story hour room for children's programming; increased space for library users, including quiet study areas; more space for books and other loan materials; more office and storage space for processing books; a new bookmobile garage; and a new roof to eliminate leakage problems which have caused considerable damage to the interior of the building.

In addition to your regular campaign flyers, put together a simple fact sheet for your staff to use in answering patron questions.

Where are voters most likely to go for information about your bond issue? To the people who work in the library, of course. And they aren't going to wander all the way back to the director's office to do it, either. They're going to ask the person who's checking out their books, or looking up an address for them, or shelving in the fiction section. Everyone on your staff should be able to answer such basic questions as, "What do you need a new building for?", "How much is this going to cost me?", and "You aren't going to paint over those lovely old murals, are you?"

Put together a simple fact sheet and see that everyone on the staff gets a copy. And leave extras at the public service desks to give out.

 If your bond issue must pass in outlying areas, create a separate flyer detailing the benefits to these areas.

There always seems to be rivalry between the people at the county seat and those in other towns and regions of the county. People resent being taxed for things they don't use. If a library issue must be voted on by those who are served by branches and book-mobiles, these voters must be made to understand how an improved main library will benefit them.

Patrons cannot be expected to realize that a larger processing area will mean that books will get to their branches faster, or that an improved reference collection will speed the answers to their questions. You must tell them, in so many words, that this issue will be worth their tax dollars.

 Try to use social and civic groups to distribute flyers and yard signs.

Local club groups are always looking for community service projects to perform. They have a large supply of energy and enthusiasm just waiting to be channeled. Often the hardest part of an election campaign is simply delivering the signs and brochures. Local groups can organize distribution within their areas under the direction of your campaign committee. They can canvass door-to-door, deliver yard signs, and even recruit new volunteers.

🏛 *Try to have at least one resident from every precinct on your campaign committee.*

As anyone who has bought Girl Scout cookies will tell you, people buy more from people they know. Your campaign committee will be talking to voters and soliciting yard signs, and they will feel more comfortable, and have better luck, if they already know these people, if only by sight.

In rural areas, distribution is much harder and takes longer simply because of the larger distances between neighbors. It may work better on a neighbor-to-neighbor basis. Churches and granges are another way to reach large numbers of people in rural areas. And don't forget the 4-H and Ruritan clubs.

🏛 *During the weeksreceding the election, display a scale model of the proposed building—if you dare!*

This is a tricky one. It can backfire on you. It is vital that you keep the public informed; voters don't like to think that someone is trying to slip them a fast one. They want to know exactly what is going on. If you don't display a model, or at least a large artist's rendering (preferably both), and if you *don't* drag these around to every club and mall in the county, and if you *don't* drown the populace in minutiae about square footage and linear feet of shelving and foot-candles, they may turn surly and accuse you of trying to pry good money out of them for a mere boondoggle.

On the other hand, if you *do* broadcast the details of the projected building, you will undoubtedly hear shrieks of dismay from those who either hate the design or fear that you will change a sacred detail of their beloved old edifice. These folks are usually a minority, but they can be a very strident one.

It may be possible to play it both ways, however. A scale model and an artist's rendering usually show only the exterior of the building. Floor plans show only the inside. Which are more likely to cause you trouble? Show the public everything you want them to see, and describe what you display in exhaustive detail. Downplay the rest of it until after the election.

🏛 ***Put together a slide/tape or video presentation on the history of your library building or system, and take it around to present to clubs and organizations.***

People are always interested in their own history, and libraries are usually chock full of it. There are bound to be old photographs of the first librarian, the dedication of the building, the Depression-era depot stations, the bookshelf at the USO, and story hours from the 1950s and 1960s. These can be interspersed with modern photos showing the crack in the foundation, the water-damaged plaster, and the reading room so crowded after school that a child is perched on the window sill. This makes a nice presentation that shows how important the library has been to the community and how much the building project is needed. Record a narrative to go with it, back the whole thing up with a Brandenburg Concerto, and you've got a program that even your shyest staff members can present. All they have to do is plug it in and push the button.

Library expansion full speed ahead

JOE MIZER

(From *The Times-Reporter*, 5-3-89, A-1, Dover-New Philadelphia, Ohio.)

It was party time in the Tuscarawas County Public Library Tuesday night.

"We're just ecstatic," said library board president James Patrick, after learning that the board's 0.3-mill bond issue was approved by a vote of 5,109 to 3,358.

It was the board's second attempt to raise $1.5 million over 20 years for a major library expansion and renovation project. The issue was defeated in last November's general election by a narrow 605-vote margin.

Patrick said Tuesday night that staff, library board and campaign committee members "just had a group meeting and everybody was jumping up and down.

"We were hoping it would pass. But I didn't expect the overwhelming passage. It was almost two to one.

"We're so happy that the others passed, too. I think it's good for the area."

Donna Schwab, chairman of the bond passage committee, also was ecstatic. "We're just thrilled that the community came out and voted for it. We're very, very happy," she said. "I feel our community is very progressive."

Head Librarian Susan Hagloch said, "We were all sitting around waiting for the results, and boy were we ever happy. I'm just so pleased and gratified at the way the community rallied behind us."

Hagloch added that her first telephone call today will be to Koster and Associates of Cleveland, the library's architect, to get the process started toward the expansion and renovation.

She said library officials have "the basic floor plan, but none of the detail work yet."

The architectural firm also will handle the bidding process for construction, which she estimates will take several months.

The project will include a 9,000-square-foot, two-story addition at the rear of the main library building on Fair Ave. NW, New Philadelphia. The addition has been designed to maintain the library's historic architectural design and will include:

- An elevator to provide total accessibility for the physically disabled.

- A meeting room for groups of up to 50 people.

- A story hour room for children's programming.

- Increased space for library users, including quiet study areas.

- More space for books and other loan materials.

- Office and storage space for processing books.

- New bookmobile garage.

- New roof to eliminate leakage problems which have caused considerable damage to the interior.

The total project is estimated at $2 million, with the additional $500,000 to be provided from the board's building fund and fund-raising events.

The levy will cost the average homeowner (one with a $50,000 property) an additional $5.25 annually.

The Day the Roof Fell In

WILLIAM C. COOPER

(From *American Libraries*, April 1991. Copyright 1991 by ALA. Reprinted with permission.)

Even under the best of circumstances, building a new library is exciting and difficult. Coping with a building disaster might be described in the same way. My library faced both—at the same time!

The Laurens County (S.C.) Library serves some 55,000 people through a headquarters library in Laurens, the county seat with a population of 12,000, and a branch in Clinton, the county's other major town. By the mid-1980s, our 10,500-sq.-ft. headquarters, erected in 1940 with WPA funds, had become totally inadequate.

In February 1984 the library board received the recommendation from its building consultant that a new 23,000-sq.-ft. library should be built. The recommendation was presented to the county council, but lack of funding put the plan on the back burner.

Late in 1985, a local family offered to donate a tract of land in an excellent location for the site of the new library. The one string attached to this gift was that funding for the new facility had to be available and a contract let within two-and-one-half years. Not a long time to design a building and raise $1.5 million!

An architectural firm was retained, the exterior of the building was designed, and a model was built. Arranging and designing the interior would come later—funding the project had to be addressed immediately! Although a major portion of the money would have to come from the county if the project was to fly, there was practically no chance of total public funding. Public and private financing would have to be combined.

Cockroach wants you!

A volunteer fundraising chairperson, who fully appreciated the need for the new library, was civic-minded, well-known, and people-oriented, was needed immediately. Fortunately, the person who met these requirements was a native son, a retired marine officer, and the vice-president of a locally owned bank. Best of all, he agreed to accept the responsibility!

The benefits of lobbying county and city officials became clear in the fall of 1986 when county council included $800,000 in a capital improvements bond issue for the new library building. The naysayers, who always surface when a project such as this is proposed, were now having to retract their predictions of doom! One of our regular library patrons, an octogenarian, told me very early in the project that I was either a "damned fool" or "crazy" to be proposing this library project in our county. I was determined to show him I was neither.

With a site, a plan, an $800,000 commitment from the county, and the near-certainty of an additional $150,000 LSCA grant, a new library was almost a sure thing!

Private fundraising efforts included contacting individuals, businesses, and foundations. The building model was placed in stores, churches, and other public areas. Library supporters and library staff used the model often with the many programs we presented to civic clubs throughout the county. We became experts at moving the model through narrow doors, up and down stairways that had landings at midpoint, and into small elevators.

"Cockroach wants you to join the Add-A-Brick Bunch!" announced bookmarks and posters. County school children were targeted with a campaign endorsed by Carl Anthony Payne, better known as "Cockroach" to fans of "The Cosby Show." Payne is from Laurens County and has relatives there. The children were pleased with the bookmarks and posters displaying Cockroach's picture.

A branch disaster

On September 14, 1987, when workmen arrived at the Clinton branch to repair what appeared to be a problem with the ceiling, the new library became secondary. The workmen discovered that the entire roofing structure of the building was near collapse; the roof trusses had failed. Just weeks earlier, over 50 children had sat under that roof attending a summer reading program. The building was immediately evacuated and closed.

We'd read of fires and earthquakes, floods, and vandalism, but not of 13-year-old buildings falling in with no apparent cause. It was a totally helpless feeling—not knowing what caused the roof trusses to sever or what the repairs would entail. Would the entire contents of the building have to be removed? How long would the library be closed?

Soon we learned that the entire book collection would have to be packed and stored along with all the furnishings and shelving. Repairs would take many months. A roofing engineer said the problem was the result of a flawed structural design. Simply put, the roofing system had not been designed to provide proper support.

Overnight, our priorities were shifted from raising funds and designing the new building in Laurens to coping with a disintegrating building in Clinton.

Arrangements had to be made to maintain service for Clinton residents. The public meeting room in city hall was reserved for weekly story hours. A church near the library provided space to set up a small reading room for newspapers, magazines, and best sellers. The bookmobile parked at the church three days a week. Patrons were encouraged to phone requests to the main library in Laurens so wanted items could be delivered by the bookmobile.

Temporary supports were placed in the library building to make it safe for the staff to pack the collection of over 20,000 volumes. A moving company was hired to remove all the boxes of books, shelving, equipment, and furniture and store them in a safe place with adequate insurance.

And yes, the fundraising effort for the new headquarters library continued.

On May 8, 1988, the Clinton Public Library, roof properly supported and brightened by new carpeting, paint, and reupholstered furniture, was reopened. I wouldn't recommend this as a way to give your library a facelift!

Several weeks later ground was broken for the new main library. 1987 had proven to be one hell of a year. 1988 promised to be better.

The new Laurens County Library officially opened to the public on November 21, 1989. Since an out-of-court settlement could not be reached, a lawsuit has been filed against the architects and engineers who designed the Clinton Public Library and the company that manufactured the roof truss system. This suit is an attempt to recover the cost of repairs and the expenses involved with vacating the building and storing the contents.

At the Laurens County Library we've had enough experience with library construction and moving to last a lifetime.

A final note: The octogenarian who told me I was a "damned fool" is now 90 and a frequent user of our new library.

_____

William C. Cooper, director of the Laurens County (South Carolina) Library, grew up in Laurens.

3

Preparing for Construction

▥ *Be sure that every person on your staff has input during the design phase.*

No building is ever perfect, but too many buildings seem to be designed only to be looked at, not to be used. Libraries appear to be particularly prone to this problem. This one has no storage space; in that one, the children's programming area isn't closed off, and tiny shrieks penetrate every corner. I know of one metropolitan library whose computer room was built with no air-conditioning ducts. The omission wasn't noticed until summer, some months after the final punch-check.

The people who know the most about what is needed in a library are those who work there. The architect should consult with them before the design is even begun. Ideally, employees should provide input on the design of their individual work spaces. If your staff is large, this may be difficult. The architect might attend departmental meetings. Have your staff jot down what they need before the meeting, to save time. At the very least, one representative of each department's desk and programming staff should be involved, along with the department head. Don't forget the janitor! And the bookmobile personnel should have some input as to the garage design.

Some things that people want will be impossible to provide. And some things will have to be sacrificed for the sake of others. But the staff will feel that the design is, in part, their own, and that their experience and expertise are valued. This will be a big help to morale—and when construction starts, you're going to need all the morale you can muster.

Several articles in this book address the design phase. See "Library Design: The Next Generation" (p. 7), "Be Careful What You Wish For" (p. 37), "Trust Your Experience" (p. 41), "Planning a Library in One Week" (p. 4), "The Day the Roof Fell In" (p. 20), and "Setting Your House in Order" (p. 32).

Familiarize yourself with proper bidding procedures and escrow fund requirements, and prevailing wage policies and procedures.

You will almost certainly be required to bid out construction contracts. You will be responsible for being sure that all the proper forms and timetables are used. Your architects should be aware of all of this, but if they have never done a library project before, they may know no more about it than you do, as private-sector requirements are very different. This is another good reason for hiring an architect with library experience because if anything goes wrong, you and your board will be blamed. Not only would this be very bad public relations, but it could also result in lawsuits, civil citations, and large fines.

Have your building tested for asbestos at least a year before you plan to start construction.

Many public buildings, especially those built between 1950 and 1970, have asbestos in them somewhere. If you're planning any construction work in those areas, you'll have to have it either removed or encapsulated before your contractors can begin work. The sooner you get going on this, the less likely it will be to cause delays.

If you're required to accepted the "lowest responsible bid," be sure you understand what constitutes a responsible bid. You may know that a firm has a reputation for bidding low, then cutting corners to save money, but unless you can document that reputation, you're bound to accept the bid.

Check your board of trustees for any conflicts of interest before bidding begins. Such individuals should resign. Merely abstaining from a vote is not enough to avoid charges of favoritism.

If anyone on your board has *any* connection with a contracting company, it is best if that person resigns before bids are solicited. Even if their firm is not planning to bid, it is still advisable. Contractors know other contractors, and lawsuits have been filed because a bidder lost a job to someone he claimed was known to a trustee.

 Check with your local fire department about what kind of automatic fire alarm they can handle.

Several kinds of automatic fire alarms notify the fire department directly when your local alarm goes off. Be sure that your fire department can handle the kind you want to install.

 Establish written policies concerning forced closings and other personnel matters before construction begins.

There will be a number of times during construction when you'll have to shut down the library and send staff home. Before that happens, you'll want to establish what your policies are. Will staff be paid as if you had been open? Will part-time staff be allowed to make up lost hours later on? If the closing is sudden and unexpected, what about those who are off on vacation or sick leave that day? Will they still have to use their vacation time or sick leave time, or will they get the day off like everyone else?

Your project may include a period of construction when you know the library will have to be closed. Do *not* plan to have everyone take vacation then. Nothing in construction ever happens at the scheduled time. The last thing you want is for the week's closing to be postponed and all your staff gone to the beach.

Try to keep things as simple and normal as possible. It would be best to pay people as if the library were open. This simplifies your bookkeeping, and it also helps morale.

🏛 **Check with your insurance agent to see what extra coverage you will need and when you will need it.**

You'll probably need to buy builder's risk insurance. This would also be a good time to check your liability coverage, *before* someone gets clunked with falling masonry.

🏛 **Ruthlessly weed the entire collection, and clean house from top to bottom.**

Once the contractors arrive, you'll be moving a lot of things around. Depending upon the scope of your project, you could be moving everything in the building at least twice. Think about that for a minute! Certain areas may have to be moved even more often. But every item that gets thrown away is one that won't have to be moved. This knowledge may encourage even the most die-hard packrats on your staff to clear the junk out.

If you can, time your weed to coincide with the Friends' annual book sale. If you don't have a Friends group, plan your own sale. This will get the public interested in your project and prepare them for the shocks to come.

🏛 **Begin now to consider what extra staff you will need to cover your additional space, so that you can budget for them.**

Library funding is not very predictable, but if you know well in advance that your new building will require extra staff, you can say so in your budget request and—perhaps—have the funds to hire them when the time comes.

🏛 **Buy a camcorder and learn how to uthese it.**

Wouldn't it be nice to have a video record of the entire construction project? You may think you will never forget all this, but you will. If your library already has a camcorder, you want it to be available when something interesting happens, so buy another, or take the one you have out of circulation. And learn how to use it. The day the bulldozers arrive is not the time to be trying to figure out where the zoom control is.

Consider moving your clerk-treasurer off site for the duration.

Picture this: Your clerk-treasurer is inputting the new year's payroll information. The save process is just beginning. Suddenly the electrician shuts down the power to the whole building. All the information has to be input again, and payday is delayed.

Libraries are full of computers, but none is dearer to our hearts than the one that prints our paychecks. Also, construction is deadly to computers. There is dust in profusion, air conditioning doesn't work, and roof leaks are commonplace. Some computers cannot be moved, but a clerk-treasurer's setup is usually self-contained. If you can, move this office out of the building. A rented room will provide reasonable safety, as well as peace and quiet for this demanding job. Also, a rented room is a dandy place to store stuff.

 ### *Purchase smocks for staff to wear during your preparatory house cleaning and during construction.*

You will suspend your dress code while you're under construction, but even jeans and shirts should be tidy. You can order smocks for those doing grimy work, especially if they'll be serving the public later in the day. We chose different colors for each department and had the employees' names embroidered on them. It was another little lift to morale.

If you don't already have one, buy a fax machine now.

Contractors and architects find these machines almost as useful as librarians do, and they're surprisingly tough. Ours was discovered to be sitting in an inch of water one grim morning, but it survived just fine.

Try to find volunteer labor for moving offices.

If you're moving your clerk-treasurer or bookmobile off site, check with your local Boy Scouts to see if anyone is looking for an Eagle Scout project. The boy doing the project is responsible for recruiting helpers, which will save you time as well as money. If you provide a rental truck and some hand trucks, they can move an entire office in an hour. All you'll need to do is tell them where to put things. Often they will volunteer to come back any time during the project when you might need them. These boys are always full of energy and lots of fun to have around. They can lighten your load considerably.

If no Scouts are available, try your local juvenile court. Sometimes youngsters are sentenced to perform community service. The court will provide an officer or caseworker to supervise. These kids may not be as cheerful or as fast as the Scouts, but they will get the job done for you.

 ### Buy a lot of plastic sheeting to have on hand.

If you've never been involved in a construction project, you'll have no idea of the amount of dust involved. People will tell you, but you won't believe it—until the day you pat a coworker on the back in bright sunshine and see a cloud of dust rise off her shoulder. It's a fine powder that sifts into everything. At the end of the day you'll be able to write your name on your desktop. All your shoes become the same grayish brown color.

All your equipment needs to be protected as much as possible, especially computers. You can't hope to keep them entirely dust-free—they will still need to be vacuumed frequently—but plastic sheeting will help.

And one thundery day you may walk into your library to find that the roofer has blundered, and it is raining in the stacks. There are few sights so appalling as that of water pouring out of every light fixture, from Large Print all the way over to Biographies. In this sort of case, plastic sheeting is a blessing.

If you must handle any bids without assistance from the architect (e.g., phone or computer systems), be sure to go over the specifications with the successful bidder, item by item, before the contract is signed.

It is the architect's job to be sure that the contractors follow the specifications, but this only applies to the specs that they have drawn up. If you're having a new phone or computer system installed as part of your project, you'll be dealing with these contractors yourself. If at all possible, hire a consultant to work with you to decide what you want and to write the specifications. Different vendors may use different descriptive terms, so you must be sure that both you and your contractor know exactly what you expect to get.

Be aware of, and have contingency plans ready for, any employees with physical problems that might be aggravated by construction.

An employee with a respiratory condition is probably going to have trouble during construction. Those who cannot easily walk or climb stairs may not be able to manage. Those with hearing problems will find it harder to work with the public because of the extra noise. It is your responsibility to provide reasonable accommodations for these conditions, so you must have a plan for such employees.

This is another good reason for having a rented office for the clerk-treasurer. It provides a "safe house" for employees who cannot work in the library on a particular day. Here people can do secretarial tasks, cut out figures or craft pieces for children's programs, or prepare book orders. Additionally, those who cannot work near the construction might be transferred to the branches or bookmobile. This kind of personnel shift should be planned well in advance.

 Have your architect explain the standard contracts before you hire contractors. What are your responsibilities as owner?

Most architects and contractors use the standard American Institute of Architects (AIA) contracts. These, of course, are written in legalese, with a smattering of constructionese. Take some time with your architect to be sure that you understand what your responsibilities are. You may be expected to provide certain permits, proof that the building is asbestos-free, and specific insurance coverage. You'll also want to know what the contractor will and will not be doing.

 Develop a plan for the disposal of surplus furnishings and equipment.

One of the nicest things about a building renovation is that you can finally get rid of those ratty old furnishings. Most libraries accumulate a hodgepodge of different styles and colors over the years, because we buy frugally, often second-hand. A dark oak desk from the 1930s sits near a blond wood desk from the 1950s and a green metal desk from the 1960s. The sofa in the reading room was donated by the children's librarian when she redecorated her living room. *Architectural Digest* it's not.

All this junk will be jettisoned to make room for brand new stuff. What are you going to do with it?

Ideally, all of these things will go into storage, and you can have a huge auction when the project is finished. If you can afford the space, and if you can find people to transport the stuff to the space as it is removed, this will provide everyone with an equal chance at what they want, and it will also give your library a nice little nest egg.

If you can't manage this, or if you don't think of it in time—as we didn't—you will find yourself with a lot of junk to dispose of and a lot of people who want it. How will you decide what to charge? How will you be sure that things are removed in a timely fashion? The contractors cannot wait around for days on end until someone's brother-in-law brings over a truck and carries out those dismantled shelves. They want everything cleared out the minute it's no longer needed.

We gave all of our leftovers to our staff association. They held an auction that was open to staff and trustees only. We kept a list of who had bought what, and, as the item came due for removal, we could notify the purchaser right then and allow them work time to remove it that day. Most of our removal was done during the summer, and we were able to keep a stable of teenagers with pickup trucks on call.

Mark each item with a tag number and print up a list before the auction is held, so everyone will have a chance to look at everything ahead of time. Anything that is left over can be offered to the construction workers for free. Probably you will get rid of everything.

▥ *Expect trouble. You won't be disappointed.*

Librarians like things to be orderly, well-planned, and predictable. That's why a building project is so traumatic to us. Nothing happens when it's supposed to happen, and something unforeseen is always popping up.

You must expect glitches. They are part of the package. However, you'll cope. You and your staff are more flexible than you think you are, and sometimes a major hassle can turn out to be a good thing.

We had the good fortune to break ground at the start of what turned out to be the rainiest summer ever recorded in Ohio. Construction was delayed. We had leaks in profusion. The mud was horrendous. We had told the architect of our long-term problems with the city's storm sewer backing up and overflowing our ground floor window wells. He designed an overflow tank for us, with a pump that would send the water back into the sewer system gradually after a storm. We soon learned that the tank was not large enough to handle the volume of water it would receive during thunderstorms. Every time we had a major rainstorm, the plumber and the general contractor and the architect would survey the overflow and calculate possible solutions. There were sufficient thunderstorms that summer to provide a thorough study of the problem—and our staff had to mop up after each one. Ultimately, we had to spend an extra $20,000 to construct our own private storm sewer system, with six dry-wells buried under the lawns and parking lot. It was very upsetting, but not nearly as much as it would have been if we had discovered it after the project was complete. Read about someone else's problems in the article "Not Even Garlic Can Drive Bad Luck Away . . ." (p. 49). And you think you've got trouble!

 ### *Don't lose your sense of humor.*

A lot of absurdities are connected with a project like this. You have to put up with a lot of pressure and responsibility, which means a lot of headaches. You'd better get as many laughs as you can along the way. You'll need them.

Setting Your House in Order

ROBERT H. ROHLF

(From *American Libraries*, April 1989. Copyright 1989 by ALA. Reprinted with permission.)

One of the clichés of architecture is "form follows function." Librarians for several decades have *defined* function quite well and have also been able to describe it, area by area, to architectural planners. Yet an unresolved question in far too many new buildings is: how do we *arrange* those functions and locate them with the users in mind? What premises, principles, or basic guidelines do we follow to achieve the kind of library we all talk about, but too seldom see? While the comments which follow are meant primarily for public libraries, they can easily be applied to other types.

The first principle of good library planning should be that the building must be user friendly—with services located for user convenience and staff efficiency. Other principles of planning then follow. In addition, we should strive for functionality balanced with design. To achieve this goal, several criteria should be used for the location of public service points.

Public service points, regardless of type of service, should be:

- located in a consistent fashion throughout the building;

- easily accessible to users;

- easily recognizable;

- easily used;

- located in a manner that recognizes the difference between long-term and short-term users;

- located with collections and user stations, such as microform machines, to maximize staff efficiencies.

To apply these principles, develop an optimal building plan which represents the most efficient way for staff and public to use the building and to move through it. When developing plans, work from a square or a rectangle. Consulting and operating experience has shown that a rectangle with central service points usually best meets the principles. This does not limit the building to a plain, rectangular shape. Architects can create very interesting shapes and forms which are variations of basic rectangles. Nor does it mean that the rectangle should be broken into unnecessary, multiple rooms and obscure, semi-hidden areas to give a feeling of intimacy and comfort, as opposed to large, perhaps noisy, and sometimes intimidating spaces. Good design accomplishes efficiency and attractiveness, but it must follow function.

Optimal floor size

A second element in basic planning is floor size. There are practical limitations to floor sizes in a public service institution. With an optimum shape, 50,000 square feet per floor approaches the maximum, ideal public service floor size for a library. In libraries operated from a single information/reference desk, or in departmental libraries with subject-service desks, the problems of size begin to be felt at approximately 30,000 square feet of floor space. As floors increase in size, problems for staff and users increase. Excessive walking distance, confusing arrangements, and even disoriented users are possible hazards. For staff, walking distances from service points to collections, materials, and readers' spaces become tiring and grossly inefficient, increasing the time needed to actually serve the public.

Hubs of service

There are only so many optimal arrangements which make any sense. Perhaps one can best plan a service desk by remembering the function of that desk and how it must relate to areas or collections around it. A public service desk—whether an information desk, young adult service desk, or youth services desk—should resemble the hub of a wheel with collections, indexes, special equipment, and readers' spaces emanating like spokes from that hub. In a well-planned library, service desks become a series of spokes and hubs, each one touching on the other in a manner which is easy to access, easily recognizable, and consistently located. These principles apply to single- or multiple-floor buildings.

Operational efficiency is another strategy which must be developed by the library planner. Operational efficiency is that which connects staff work areas with service points, locates collections easily accessible to the staff as well as to the public, and places user-operated equipment such as computers, CD-ROM readers, and microform readers in areas easily observable by staff. Operational efficiency relates to how a library is used, not necessarily how it should look in the abstract. With these general principles and admittedly biased opinions in mind let us review some of the questions planners should ask themselves when developing locations and spaces for a public library.

Pertinent Questions

When one develops a service desk, will the user be able to see it from a distance, or will it be obscured by building structure, non-related signs, or architectural features such as display areas or sculpture? Can the public easily see an area they wish to approach? Is its access logical and easy to determine? Using the general information/reference desk as an example, is its location easily discernible after one is past the circulation function? Can one approach it without feeling intimidated; or is it designed in such a way that users may feel they are bothering the staff, rather than approaching them for assistance? Is the desk designed to promote the reference interview as a normal and logical outcome of the surroundings?

Is the information desk located near the reference collection? Are major parts of the collection which the information and reference staff will be using near the desk? In short, is the desk logically located within the general traffic patterns of the building and are the collection materials easily accessible?

Prudent planners will ask themselves some additional questions: What parts of the collection or other service desks relate to this information desk, and how are they located in relation to it? Does the building plan allow for an easily visible and accessible traffic pattern from the information desk to other parts of the collection or to other special services, or are the sight lines and traffic patterns obscure and convoluted? Do architectural elements interfere with logical movement or do they aid the user in moving from one area to another?

A common problem of contemporary public library planning is the failure to arrange collections so that they flow in a logical sequence and allow the unassisted reader to find material. Building shapes and configurations should allow for flexible shelving locations and logical collection shelving flow. Forcing collections and shelving to meet some architectural design element which results in disjointed shelving, disoriented users, and illogical collection arrangements benefits no one.

Short- and long-term users

Planners should carefully analyze services and collections for short- and long-term users. One finds this in many library situations where "popular materials" are located near the door and the information and reference function are further into the building or even on an upper or lower floor. This arrangement assumes that people looking for information and reference assistance are willing to go further into the building to have their needs met than are those simply seeking leisure materials.

Good library planning recognizes how people use the library and how they wish to be convenienced rather than inconvenienced. It parallels the retail concept where "impulse" items are generally located near the entrances and larger, more expensive items are located in the building's interior.

Logical mingling

Plan to accommodate readers to avoid totally controlled, mass-reading areas that are too often placed in the central areas of the buildings near service desks. Unfortunately, most of the noise of library activities occurs here. Readers should have quiet areas for reading and study, and users of the collection should not be forced to walk through rows and rows of readers in order to get to the shelves. Chairs and tables should be available within a reasonable distance from any part of the collection. Shelving and readers should be intermingled in a logical, convenient fashion so that readers should never have to go more than 40 or 50 feet to find a seat.

Too many libraries have been planned on the assumption that readers must be kept close to service desks and under the eyes of the staff, and collections can be placed around the perimeter of the building or at some distance from service desks and reader stations. Good library planning recognizes that readers also deserve the perimeters of the building where they can find some modicum of quiet. It also recognizes that people scanning the collection should be able to reach it without having to walk through the entire library to get to perimeter walls or bays. Far too often, architectural forms such as dropped ceilings and changes in lighting have dictated arrangements. In following the frequently found "spine" concept of architectural form, readers are lined up through the width or length of the building with collections surrounding the outside walls. All persons entering and exiting the building are forced to walk by readers' seats to reach the collection. This is a disservice to the reader and the short-term user.

Through users' eyes

How a user might find and approach service points and collections, and how staff might interact with users and each other must be foremost in the planner's mind. Have library staff members go through the plan as though they were users. Are desks visible and approachable? Are desks located in consistent fashion; that is, are all the desks located as the user might approach them or are some hidden, remote and perhaps even unrecognizable? Are proposed graphics clear, legible, and yet not overwhelming in number? Is the relationship of service points logical, clear, and staff-efficient? Are collections accessible to the public service staff without unusual, illogical, or extraordinary distances required simply because of the design of the building? Can one use the building without having to disturb readers?

Having staff members analyze use patterns will achieve increased efficiencies and easier-to-use library buildings.

The form of the building must follow the function and layout of service points and service areas. Service areas, collection arrangement, and reader spaces must not be squeezed into unusual, unnecessary, or arbitrary spaces and shapes. Foremost must be the ability of a non-library user to approach and recognize service points and overall library resources. When the architecture inhibits the library user, the building is a failure.

Robert H. Rohlf is director of Hennepin County (Minnesota) Public Library and principal partner of Professional Library Consultants, P.A. Formerly building planning coordinator for the Library of Congress, he has consulted on over 100 library building projects.

Be Careful What You Wish For: The Biloxi Library and Cultural Center

CHARLINE LONGINO

(From *Mississippi Libraries*, Summer 1991. Copyright 1991 by *Mississippi Libraries*. Reprinted with permission.)

The library wanted more space for books and people to work; more space for children's programs and book talks; more space for art shows and music recitals; more space to grow.

The city wanted a landmark; "a memorable downtown focal point," a complex that "respects the history of the community, but is as modern as tomorrow."

The community wanted a comfortable place to read where there would be room to check out their books, hold their club meetings, and send their kids to story hours.

The result of all this wanting was the design and construction of the new Biloxi Library and Cultural Center. And, just like in the fairy tales, everyone's wishes came true. Also, just like in the fairy tales, everyone learned that you have to be careful what you wish for . . . .

Since 1926, generations of kids had slid down the wide banisters of the cracked concrete stairs to the old library. Generations had attended story hour, browsed the stacks and done homework at the old wooden library tables, listened to poetry readings and choral programs, and sometimes, napped in the sun by an age-bubbled window.

By the early 1970s, hurricanes, age, and those generations of Biloxians had taken a heavy toll. Where once the old two-story building had swallowed the library and still provided space for Red Cross and King's Daughters, and practically every cultural organization in town, now the entire building bulged with books. Boxes of books sat on the stairs. Towers of books leaned precariously from every surface. Even the workroom space necessary for processing the books had been crowded out by book storage.

On a larger scale, the old downtown of Biloxi was facing a similar toll of age and of the overwhelmingly successful, commercial competition of the mall. The city needed something to bring people back downtown and the city needed a new library. Thus was born the Biloxi Design Festival.

Six nationally known architects and 32 students from five area schools of architecture were invited to a five day design marathon. Each architect and his team of students were presented the same situation—to design a library and museum for the city of Biloxi on a recently purchased area in the block directly across the street from City Hall. The local newspaper and television station were given every opportunity to conduct interviews and observe the design process, and they provided continuing coverage of the affair. City officials and the community were encouraged to tour the work areas and discuss the project with the architectural teams. Finally, more than 400 people attended a public presentation of each team's final design.

The most dramatic design among the six came from the team headed by William Turnbull of MLTW/Turnbull Associates in San Francisco. He, along with Art Kaple of the Louisiana State University faculty and students from Mississippi State, Auburn, and Tulane, presented a building with a high sloping roof and wings that reached to embrace a courtyard plaza where the city's original library, a wood-framed cottage, could be relocated. City officials liked the design so well that they presented Turnbull with the commission for the Library and Cultural Center building.

In October 1975, a ground-breaking ceremony was held for the contest-named Biloxi Bibliotheque et Musee. The mayor announced that plans called for completion of the project in one year's time and that Senator John C. Stennis would speak at the dedication. Unfortunately, that "bright, sunshiny day" was not an omen of the weather to come. When it rains on the coast, it rains in torrents, and the water slowed construction again and again. The wet and sandy base soil had to be firmed with pilings driven into the ground. In October of 1976 on a windy, rainy day, the city's two high school bands played, city officials expressed pleasure in the "unveiling" of the new Library and Cultural Center, and Senator Stennis dedicated the new building. On July 5, 1977, the community was invited "to attend the formal opening of Biloxi's newest landmark, and the inauguration of city officials." In August, library staff started moving books and magazines, papers, films and historical records to the new structure. Moving, as the local paper described it, was like going from the broom closet to the Taj Mahal. On September 11, 1977, the library was again formally and finally opened to the public.

The Biloxi Library and Cultural Center made the cover of the *Architectural Record* with a six page spread of photographs, diagrams and narrative. The *AIA Journal*, the official magazine of the American Institute of Architects, devoted another six pages and titled it "An Evocative Enclosure of Luminous Space." *American Libraries* also used the library for its cover photo and the American Library Association presented a Merit Award for the design. The city had gotten its wished-for landmark.

All these prestigious organizations attempted to describe the building that resulted from Turnbull's design. The architect, himself, spoke of the metaphor of the garden wall.

> Where do people want to read? By the window in the sunshine. It needed intimate scale, a garden outlook, light. In the city you make a garden with a wall around it. What could we make a wall out of? . . . books. So it is

a hollow wall—books on one edge, garden on the other. The meeting rooms, museums, etc., hang off the back. For the control place in between, there is the one piece of clear geometry. We put the cottage in the garden as a monument. *AIA Journal* described the building as a sort of push me/pull you with pincers. On one side, the library's entrance and segmented arms frame a courtyard, which it shares with the neo-classical city hall across the street . . . on the other side is a high observation tower forming a 65-foot entrance foyer for the cultural center. Inside, the library and center are linked—and kept separate—by a rotunda in which an octagonal circulation desk acts as a control point. Everything has been done to give a domestic scale and setting, which is transformed by light into something quite special.

Indeed, one thing all observers seem to return to in describing the Library and Cultural Center is the manner in which the building plays with light. Wall-size windows surround the courtyard side of the library wings. Skylights line the ridges of the roof and more skylights make a huge circle of light over the rotunda in the center of the building. The light washes in and is filtered by the cool color scheme of whites and grays, aquas and lavenders. The result is a "hushed atmosphere," a "refreshing antidote to the hot and humid climate . . . a soft, sustained mood."

The building was and is a magnificent piece of art. Although the Cultural Center and its plaza have not alone been enough to save the downtown business area, it has become, as the city hoped, a focal point for city activities that range from Mardi Gras parades to Christmas tree lightings to city inaugurations. After 13 and a half years, in a building with 33,400 square feet, the library still has ample space for its work, for books and materials, and for its programs. The community has willingly filled the space in two meeting rooms with clubs and boards and special meetings, and has happily adopted the library's comfortable chairs and butcher-block study tables for their own. Since 1989, the gallery spaces in the Center have been filled by the Mississippi Museum of Art whose Gulf Coast branch now occupies that quarter of the building. The museum sponsors special art exhibits and, at times, uses the building's wonderful acoustics to fill it with a wide range of music—from harpsichord to gospel singing. Just as all wished, art, music and literature are brought together under one roof. It's just that the roof leaks.

The Biloxi Library and Cultural Center was designed as a wonderful piece of sculpture, but art is not required to be utilitarian—buildings are. The interior library is a wonderful complex of angles and areas with numerous quiet nooks for reading. The first librarian in the building pointed out the security problems arising when staff cannot see nor hear what is happening in all areas, and those problems have continued to the current day. Despite staff care and closing procedures, members of the public, both junior and senior, still get themselves locked in the building after hours. In addition, the opportunities for graffiti in the far wings of the building have not been lost on several generations of teenagers. The wonderful acoustics resulting from all that open space and high ceilings also mean that the sounds of story hour can annoy patrons upstairs on the Genealogy balcony and quiet questioning at the front desk can be heard clearly 60 feet away at the study tables.

The Center, like most public buildings in the past twenty years, was designed for climate control. No windows open or close; no fans stir the air. Temperature is dependent on ducts and valves, chillers and cooling towers, compressors and furnaces. The library furnace has never failed. Unfortunately, in a climate that often requires cooling equipment from late February through early November, all of the other items on this list have, some frequently. After less than ten years, the chillers and cooling tower for the building had to be replaced at city expense. Currently, the building's compressor is under repair. There is still considerable discussion regarding blame—whether construction and materials are at fault, or the building design taxes the capacity of its climate control.

The roof which stretches like a series of metal tents over the entire building is the most notable feature of the exterior. Over the years it has gained quite a bit of attention on the interior as well. People expect drips and puddles outside when it rains; they are not so sanguine when the same occurs inside. Shortly after the library opened, staff noted that when it rained hard, wet spots were showing in the ceiling. The ridge-line skylights, which do so much to provide that "luminous" quality to the building, also appear to be the culprits in providing that damp quality. Varying and expensive efforts over the years have sought to correct the problem. Currently, the City of Biloxi is mulling a proposal to "finally and completely" correct the situation. It is estimated that it will cost somewhere between one hundred thousand and a quarter of a million dollars. In the meantime, the library has taken up the fashion of draping some of its book stacks in clear plastic and manning the buckets when the rain falls. Again, no one has conclusively assigned blame to construction or design.

Still, while engineers consult and city fathers consider funding sources, the library continues. Coast visitors still compliment the staff on their "new" library; troops of children march in for story hours, puppet shows and summer reading programs; more and more books and tapes and videos circulate; and the library regulars sit in the comfortable wingback chairs reading and, sometimes, napping in the sun.

_____

Charline Longino is Head Librarian, Biloxi (Mississippi) Public Library.

Trust Your Experience

NORA RAWLINSON, EDITOR

(From *Library Journal*, December 1990. Copyright 1990 by *Library Journal*. Reprinted with permission.)

Dazzled by a beautiful new library, I found myself echoing the words of the 1989 judge for the American Institute of Architects/American Library Association (AIA/ALA) Award, who said: "the symmetry of the concept and the sophistication of the façades give the library an exterior serenity."

Wandering around the breathtaking edifice, I realized that something was bothering me. As the proud director led the tour, it struck me that the building had taken priority over the collections and services it contained. Even an inveterate book lover like me found no enticement from the shiny new books. There were other problems. The building was a security nightmare. Dozens of nooks and crannies waited to hide nefarious activities from scrutiny. In fact, when the building was opened for the dedication ceremonies, the staff had to first eject an encampment of homeless men.

Anyone who had ever worked a public service desk would have insisted on clear sight lines throughout the building. The most cursory community analysis would have revealed that the site was near a local gathering point for the homeless.

The sad truth is that many library directors and architects ignore their own best building consultants: the staff.

I was once a member of a library staff committee planning a workable interior for a new branch. A clerical supervisor wrote up the specifications for the charging desk. The result was a desk that required few wasted steps, where the pencils and scrap paper were always where you needed them.

The committee decided that children's shelving needed to be reversed. Commercially available shelving used the top for display and the bottom for storage, forcing adults to crawl around on the floor, and removing face-out books from a child's-eye view. We designed our own custom shelving with display bins on the floor, so a child could plop down and browse happily. Spine-out shelving was at the top, where an adult could locate the desired version of *Snow White* without back strain.

We have all heard of library architectural disasters: a children's section opening onto a lovely, but hazardous mezzanine, a roaring heat duct located right above the information desk. Such stories help create lucrative incomes for library building consultants, but no consultant can be as practical, or locally responsive, as the staff itself.

The field lacks practical tips, but there is a *Checklist of Library Building Design Considerations*, published by ALA's Library Administration and Management Association's Buildings and Equipment Section. One of the items on this list of questions to ask during the design process is, "Are there areas where patrons can be undetected within the library at closing time?" The architect for the building I visited obviously thought the desirable answer was "Yes."

The 1988 edition of the *Checklist* is a mixed bag, ranging from overly broad philosophical considerations ("Is the building visually satisfying to look at?") to the outright perplexing ("Is there an art gallery?"). A new edition, planned for this month, includes revisions of 25 percent of the material. Even in its present form, it is more meaningful than any architectural treatise on libraries.

Reading what architects have to say about libraries can be profoundly disturbing. They harbor as many incorrect beliefs and prejudices about libraries as other nonusers. One architect, commenting on the elements of good library design in a recent issue of *Library Administration & Management*, asserted that there should be "no distracting sound or noticeable air movement . . . [all spaces must be] wrapped with the appropriate 'quiet.' " Can any public service librarian read that without guffawing?

Give your architect a nice plaque to hang over the drawing board, inscribed,

A library should be a practical thing to be used,
not an ideal to be admired.

—Charles Cutter, *LJ*, February 1901

4

Construction

 Suspend your dress code for the duration.

Where there's construction, there's dirt. You won't believe how much dirt! And you'll be moving around a lot of books and junk that hasn't budged in 20 years. You'll get filthy every day. Don't even think about wearing your nice silk dress-for-success suits. Stock up on jeans in a variety of colors and some cotton shirts. During the summer you won't have any air conditioning (no matter what they tell you), so allow your staff to wear shorts. You'll want to draw the line at cutoffs and flip-flops, but everyone should understand what you mean if you say "nice grubbies."

Doubtless you and the rest of the professional staff will want to dress up on days when you're speaking to the Kiwanis Club or hosting a board meeting. Be warned. Those are the days when the worst disasters happen. Be sure you have smocks, aprons, or coveralls on hand.

There is one caveat for women: After eighteen months of wearing comfortable lace-up shoes and heavy socks, it will be miserable going back to high-heeled pumps. Often your first day in such shoes will be Dedication Day, an uncomfortable day at the best of times. Keep the aspirin handy. Eventually your feet will readjust.

Follow up on staff questions and concerns as they arise.

As construction gets underway, your staff will probably start asking questions and making comments: "Shouldn't that wall be higher?" "Isn't there supposed to be a drainpipe in that corner?" "That closet looks too small!" Your initial reaction is probably, "What are you asking me for? I'm a librarian, not a contractor!" For right now, however, you are both. Your copy of the construction drawings should be handy to your desk. Sometimes you can look at them and answer the question right then. "That's the size the closet is supposed to be." "The drainpipe is on the opposite wall."

Other times you will have to take the question to the construction supervisor. If he's a good one, he will be polite about your questions, because, after all, you are paying the bills. And sometimes these questions catch genuine errors.

On the morning after the day the masonry contractors finally arrived and began building walls, one of my clerks came to me, saying, "I know I'm probably being silly, but aren't there supposed to be windows in that wall?" Surely no one could be absent-minded enough to forget windows, could they?

Yes, they could, and yes, they had. And nobody noticed it until Shirley mentioned it. They had to go back and cut the windows out. Not impossible, but time-consuming, noisy, and expensive. Sooner or later somebody on the contractors' team would have realized. But Shirley caught it first. Listen to your staff!

 Have your staff check the site every evening, after the contractors leave, to be sure everything is locked up tightly. Hire a nighttime guard if you can.

Security gets difficult when your whole north wall disappears. The contractors will put a plywood partition across the opening in the building, but they may not always remember to lock all the doors at night. Kids, curious passersby, and lost patrons may wander in. If one of them trips and falls, you could have a lawsuit on your hands. And if vandals or thieves get into the library, you'll have other problems. You'll sleep better at night if you check the entry points yourself.

A nighttime guard is a great idea if you can afford one. This person can keep out intruders and watch for electrical shorts or leaks. Be sure to give the guard your telephone number, and the construction superintendent's, in addition to those of the police and fire department. Also, you might get a break on insurance costs if you have this extra security.

🏛 *Have parties for your staff. Include the construction crew.*

There is a lot of giddy excitement at the beginning of a building project, but the glow fades quickly when your staff is working without heat (or air conditioning) and in constant noise and dust. Plan celebrations for staff birthdays, for holidays, for milestones in the project. You can figure out a way to pay for chips and pop every month or two. These little parties can do a lot for morale. Once some of our staff clubbed together to pay for an Elvis impersonator for a coworker's birthday party.

Invite the construction crews to partake of the goodies during their lunch hours. We were surprised when they told us that no one had ever done that for them before. They really appreciated it, and they showed it. These people can do a lot to make your lives easier during construction—or to make you miserable. It's best to be friends.

🏛 *Get the contractors to walk you through the new systems as they are installed. Where are the circuit breakers? Where do the furnace filters go? How do you open the elevator manually when the power goes out?*

It seems like a natural part of the contractor's job to teach you what you need to know about the system they've installed, but it's a part no one seems to have told them about. You won't really know when they're finished. They'll be there one day and gone the next. Sometimes they come back in a week or so, and sometimes they don't. It may be months before the final punch list is completed. In the meantime, you'll need to know a lot of things. When the fire alarm goes off in Zone 6, you need to know where Zone 6 is. When the HVAC system starts blasting out frigid air in January, and you call the contractors, they'll ask "Which unit is that?" But they probably never told you that you had more than one unit, much less which areas each one serves.

It saves a lot of grief if you seek out the answers to these questions while the contractor is captive on your premises. You'll want to snoop around every night to see what they've been up to, then ask questions the next day.

You may want to wait until the architect visits to ask your questions. It lends you an air of authority to walk in the architect's shadow and you have a perfect right to do so. But remember that the architect will be talking to the contractor in constructionese. You'll be lucky to understand one word in four.

Most librarians develop the habit of asking the same questions of the contractor and the architect, at separate times. You'll double your chance of 1) understanding the answer and 2) remembering it. And if you get two different answers, you know there's a problem somewhere.

 ### Order extra supplies of paint, carpet, and upholstery fabric.

When you order all your carpeting and furniture, be sure to order an extra yard of each fabric, as well as spare carpeting. Someday someone will spill or tear something, and by that time the color and pattern you chose will no longer be manufactured. Similarly, you want to be able to touch up nicks and marks on the walls yourself.

If something is delivered before the contractor arrives to install it, check yourself to see that it is what was ordered.

Often contractors for shelving, carpet, and the like will have their materials sent directly to you, timed to arrive before their installers show up. Ask for a copy of their order so you can check it against the delivery. Then, if it's incorrect, you can notify them immediately, and they can reorder right away. Then you may not have to reschedule the installer. If the error isn't caught until the installer arrives, it may mean several weeks' delay.

🏛 *Remember that some low bidders may be the lowest because they're planning to cut corners where they think it won't be noticed. Have an outside engineer check the installations periodically.*

Heaven forbid you should be accused of being suspicious, but when a contractor's crew does most of its work after 5 PM, when all the other contractors have gone home, you do wonder. When they dawdle over the duct work until after all the suspended ceilings have been hung, you can't see what's been done up there. And when someone calls the architect, the construction supervisors, and the librarian unprintable names for asking questions, you know something's fishy.

Many architects have HVAC and electrical engineers on retainer. An architect who has doubts about one of your contractors should bring one of these engineers in to check the work. If you have doubts, tell your architect you want someone brought in. Even if you have to pay for it yourself, it's cheaper than paying the contractor for garbage. And it's better than having to have a whole new system installed in five years, when this contractor has gone out of business and moved to Rio de Janeiro.

🏛 *Never believe a contractor's estimate of how long anything will take.*

I don't know whether contractors, like politicians, only tell you what they think you want to hear, or if they're just incurable optimists. I only know that no contractor's timeline that I ever heard of has come close to being met. And the architect isn't much better. You'd think they'd have a clearer idea of construction schedules than you do, but they don't seem to.

At the start of our project, the contractor estimated ten months to completion. The architect guessed fourteen. Having listened to librarians who had been through construction, I planned the dedication ceremony for sixteen months in the future. The architect was appalled. We couldn't have the dedication that late. Everyone in town would already have seen the finished project; there could be no grand unveiling. It would be an anticlimax.

Sixteen months later we had the dedication. Most of the offices and the cabinetry were still unfinished. The carpeting wasn't done. The lights were almost done. The air conditioning worked pretty well in most places. And my staff had worked all day Saturday and some of Sunday morning to get the public areas presentable. We had been closed for five weeks at that point. So it was, indeed, a grand unveiling. Some of it should have stayed veiled a little longer.

Now, as I write, it is six months later. The cabinetry was finished last week. The last light fixtures are about to be installed. The carpeting has been finished for two weeks. The heating system is somewhat improved in some places.

So when an architect and a contractor give you an estimate on time, mentally add 30 percent to it. You'll save yourself a lot of grief.

Not Even Garlic Can Drive Bad Luck Away from Norton PL

LEONARD KNIFFEL, MANAGING EDITOR

(From *American Libraries*, June 1991. Copyright 1991 by ALA. Reprinted with permission.)

At one point it got so bad that the building consultant sent Norton (Mass.) Public Library Director Robin Glasser a head of garlic "to ward off the evil spirits." But not even vampire repellent could quell the misfortune that has beset the town's 13-year-long effort to construct a replacement for its cramped 104-year-old library.

Though completed last July, the new facility remains unoccupied due to a "punch list" of needed replacements and repairs and a disagreement between the town's board of selectmen and the library board over the lease—problems that would seem solvable in a matter of months, except in Norton.

"I've been here 10 years," technical service librarian Janet Pane told *AL*, "and we've been talking about months for five of them. When we get a mover and a moving date, then I'll believe it. Up until then I won't."

Norton's problems began in 1977 when the town picked a building design and site, only to lapse into a long delay. With $2.7 million in funding in place, the project did not go out for bids until 1987 and then ended up in court, with one of the bidders insisting that the process had not been properly conducted. Meanwhile three head librarians came and went, each altering the building plan, which was discovered to have been faulty to begin with.

By last April, when Glasser became director, walls were up and plumbing and wiring were in the works. She was confident the library would be in the new building within a matter of weeks. But the troubles kept coming: Mismatched wallpaper, out-of-stock carpeting, outdated smoke detectors, an inadequate hot water system, and growing hostility between the contractor and subcontractors over payment, which strained relations between the library and the contractor.

Now in charge of the library while Glasser is out on a medical leave, Pane told *AL*, "The contractor has signed off; the library is now responsible for whatever else must be done. And the selectmen have told the board to go ahead and write up a lease and operating agreement."

The town is fed up, says Glasser. The selectmen have been flooded with letters from irate citizens, and patrons frequently vent their anger on library staff. Meanwhile, attractive upholstered chairs and oak reading tables sit waiting for Dedication Day.

"It'll be a miracle if it ever gets open and works well," says the building consultant, aptly named Patience Jackson.

Tell the World

 Plan two grand reopening parties—one for the dignitaries and one for the staff and construction crew.

You know that you'll have to have a grand dedication, with the board and the mayor and the state representatives and senators, and even national bigwigs (if you have clout enough to get them). More on this later. But you should also plan a party for the real heroes: your staff and the work crew. It should be simple: pizza and chips, pop and beer. Plan it for a Friday or Saturday night after work. Have it in the library while you're still finishing up. It's a chance for everyone to let off steam and enjoy their accomplishments, and a chance for the library to say "Thank you!"

Alternatively (or as well as, if you can afford it), take your staff out to a lunch. Choose a day toward the end of the moving-in-and-setting-up period and take everyone over to nearby restaurant. Charge it to your continuing education account—these people have been furthering their education ever since groundbreaking.

 Plan the dedication well in advance.

It is, as we all know by now, next to impossible to predict when a building project will be finished. Yet a dedication party requires a minimum of six months' planning. You'll have to choose a date pretty much by guess and by gosh. Ask the architect and the contractor when they will be done, then add two or three months to that date, depending on the size of the project.

Two articles on planning dedications are reprinted at the end of this chapter: "Library Housewarmings: Dos and Don'ts of Dedications" and "The Proper Dedication Day."

 ### *Invite the immediate universe!*

Your guest list should include every politician with constituents in your service area. Probably some of these people have helped you with funding the project, however indirectly, and they expect to be thanked. Even if they didn't, sometime in the future you may be asking them for some support, and it's wise to build relationships before you need them.

Politicians love bashes like this. They have a chance to meet their public and ally themselves to a popular local institution. Also, they're usually wonderful guests. They circulate and they keep conversation going, and this will be a help to you.

Everyone who worked on your bond issue campaign should be invited, of course. All of your Friends of the Library should be there. They can assist you with host duties, hand out programs, serve punch and cookies, and so on.

Of course, all your staff and board are invited, although some staff will have to be working. You will want someone stationed in each department who can give brief tours and answer questions, and help to clean up afterwards.

Be sure to invite other librarians. Your colleagues have been listening patiently to your tales of triumph and tribulation for months, and they'll appreciate a formal invitation to the festivities. Don't forget the state library association and the officials of the state library. Don't feel hurt if they don't come, however. Some people would rather not go visit a library on their day off, and they may figure that they'll see it later on work time. But it's polite to recognize their importance as professionals with a formal invitation.

Anyone who donated any money or effort to your project must be included. To my mind, this includes all of your loyal patrons who put up with noise, dust, and inconvenience. The simplest thing is to open up the party to the general public. This may, however, be difficult in some cases. Some libraries have a formal black-tie celebration for the official dedication, then an open-house during regular library hours.

Don't forget to invite the media! Send official invitations to the editors of the local papers as well as to the managers of all the radio and television stations.

Try to get local caterers and musicians to donate their services.

You'll want music and refreshments for your dedication, but the library may be totally broke by this time. If the Friends of the Library don't have sufficient talent in these lines, it may be possible to get local caterers and musicians to donate their services. A prominent mention in the program is good publicity for them, as is a public thank-you from the podium as part of the day's program. Of course, you'll send handwritten thank-you notes the very next day.

 Keep the dedication ceremonies short.

It is necessary to have speeches at an event like this. Your board president is entitled to a few words, and you must recognize those "without whose assistance, this project would never have been realized." But you don't have to talk everyone into a stupor. Your audience wants to look around, to visit with friends, and to munch on goodies. Half an hour should be sufficient to say what needs to be said.

If a known windbag has to be on the agenda, then cut everyone else back to a mere nod of acknowledgment. Do try to leave the windbag out.

 Send brochures offering library tours to area clubs.

Many people who are not regular library users will be curious about how their tax dollars have been spent. Some of these people can be persuaded to become regular users by going on a tour of the building. Often they haven't been in a library since they got out of school, and they don't realize how much libraries have changed.

All of the local civic and educational clubs should be offered tours. Appoint someone on your staff to coordinate these tours. Special-interest clubs might concentrate on your genealogy section, or on the Moody's and ValueLine. All the local schools should schedule class visits. The Handicapped Society will want to know what you have to offer. Scout troops, service clubs, study groups, support groups—everyone can find something tailored to their needs at the library, and this is your chance to tell them so.

If your newspaper coverage is scant, write a letter to the editor announcing your reopening and thanking everyone.

For some reason, libraries in small towns and large cities seem to get better newspaper coverage. Some newspapers seem to feel that libraries are just too boring for words. As during your bond issue campaign, you may do better if you have a strong library supporter whose business buys a lot of newspaper advertising. Get that person to call the editor.

If the paper simply won't give you the coverage you feel you're entitled to, at least you can write a letter to the editor to thank the community and to rave about your improved facility. It's better than nothing, and it might shame the paper into action.

 If you are getting a lot of new equipment or services, you may want to stagger their introduction.

If your project allows you to get a microfilm reader-printer, more CD-ROM terminals, a meeting room, or whatever, you might want to postpone some of these things for several months. That way, each one can be a separate press release.

Library Housewarmings: Dos and Don'ts of Dedications

DENNIS C. TUCKER

(From *American Libraries*, July/August 1988. Copyright 1988 by ALA. Reprinted with permission.)

The capstone to a new or remodeled library is the dedication ceremony. Promising future service as well as celebrating an achievement, the ceremony can be as formal or informal as planners choose. However, because such occasions for celebration are few and far between for libraries, organizers should make the most of the opportunity: Pull out all the stops and make the festivities as big, and as grand, as possible.

Elegance need not mean expense, though. Dedication planners may choose to celebrate economically, but should avoid any appearance of parsimoniousness or of cutting corners. Creating an impression of miserliness can harm a library's reputation.

Make a guest list

A dedication ceremony can attract new patrons to the library. Use publicity to make the general public feel welcome at the dedication. In particular, try to target people that never use the library.

Also invite everyone who is "anyone": local and county officials, state representatives, even national figures. Of course, anybody who might be even remotely connected with or interested in the library is a somebody and worth inviting. Include everyone from the new facility's architect, contractors, and vendors to library volunteers, donors, and Friends groups; representatives from library associations, the state library, and library networks; librarians and academic officers from nearby institutions; local authors; and of course, the media. When dedicating an academic library, be sure to add leaders of student government and the general student body to the guest list. Budget permitting, organizers should send formal, engraved invitations.

Although many people might not attend, personal invitations send an important two-part message to prospective guests: 1) that the library exists and 2) that its staff cares about the invitees enough to value their presence.

Set the date

Planners must permit a breathing time between moving day and the dedication ceremony. A breather between the two allows those who worked hardest on the relocation to rest and recuperate from the physical and emotional strain they have endured.

By delaying the ceremony, planners also give staff time to adjust to their new workplace, and to iron out any wrinkles in the system. Are borrowers' cards now filed in a different order or in a different location than they were in the old building? Is the periodicals collection now housed down two levels instead of up one? Because visitors will ask lots of questions on dedication day, library staffers must have time to learn the new answers.

Before putting both themselves and the library on public display, staffers can use this interval to correct any flaws or mistakes they discover after occupying the building. If books have ended up on the floor, staffers can shelve them or at least hide them in storage before the public arrives for the ceremony. Someone can mend the snag in the carpet left by the jagged wheels of the 400th dolly and replace the screws that fell out of the bottom of the chair before the mayor sits on it. Because dedication day may be the library's only day of glory until the next construction project, make sure everything is its polished best.

Delaying the dedication also gives organizers adequate time to plan the ceremony. It is a reasonably safe bet that if the staff has to concentrate on the move and dedication-day plans simultaneously, neither one will be done well. Build in extra time for unforeseen setbacks.

Conversely, don't wait so long that the shiny new building begins to show signs of wear: dirt spots on carpet, graffiti on furniture and walls, scuff marks from feet placed on those wonderfully low windowsills.

Plan to brainstorm

Planning something as complex as a dedication ceremony is best done by a committee. It takes several people with divergent ideas to put together a program truly representative of the library and its community. Include librarians and para-professionals, Friends, trustees, and a patron or two. For an academic library dedication committee, enlist faculty members, administrators, and student representatives.

The first few committee meetings should simply be brainstorming sessions. Don't discount or overrule any ideas as this stage. Anyone with any ideas at all—no matter how strange, absurd, remote, or expensive—must feel free to speak. Ideas will spark more ideas; hearing some people's ridiculous or wildly expensive notions may inspire others to suggest some brilliant and affordable alternatives.

After a few sessions, begin narrowing down the list. When only the best ideas remain, choose enough for a ceremony of reasonable length. To keep the ceremony within the bounds of human endurance, the committee may even have to discard some of their best ideas. Many otherwise impressive and inspirational ceremonies have been ruined because the planners—or the speaker—forgot that the mind can absorb only as much as the posterior can withstand.

When the committee has determined which ideas to incorporate, assign responsibilities to different members. One member, for example, might agree to invite the governor to be the dedication speaker and to contact alternates if necessary. Another might oversee physical arrangements—securing and placing tables and chairs, a public address system, etc. A third committee member might plan the refreshments.

Lure the press

Spare no effort in contacting the local media—television, radio, and newspapers—about the upcoming event. In a small town, the dedication of a new library facility could be a major feature story. Even a large city newspaper might develop it into a major story if there is a sympathetic writer or editor on staff.

Some radio and television talk shows interview guests about community concerns. Seek a spot on such a show. If neither the library director nor members of the planning committee feel at east being interviewed on the air, perhaps someone else could represent the library, such as the president of the local Friends group.

Tell the press which well-known personalities will attend and what roles the celebrities will play in the program. The local media might feel that a library dedication is unworthy of news coverage in itself, but if a VIP is to be the dedication speaker, they might reconsider.

For example, 1984 dedication ceremonies for Bethel College Library, Mishawaka, Ind., attracted representatives from all three network affiliates because Governor Robert Orr was one of the speakers. Afterward, reporters bombarded him with questions about several current political issues. That evening, television news featured the dedication briefly, but also carried several additional spots of the governor discussing the issues. Bethel's fringe benefit: The college's new library showed up very well in the background.

Entertainment and food are two drawing cards at any ceremony. People who might not otherwise come to a library dedication might be enticed there if the entertainment appeals to them. And once they have made their first visit to the library, it's much easier to get them to return.

To increase attendance, search for entertainment with wide local appeal: a puppet show or story hour for the children, a how-to session for adults, a popular local musical group for teens, a well-known author.

Any time there is an offer of free food or drink, there are also going to be those who abuse the privilege. Determine what kind of spread you can afford and what type of control to exercise.

Libraries that normally forbid food and drink in the building often relent on dedication day. Remember that vermin find the food equally attractive no matter how or when it gets there. If librarians allow food in the library during the dedication, they will have difficulty explaining to students a week later why they can't eat candy bars while studying there. Designate one area, preferably outside the library proper, for guests to enjoy food and drink, and restrict all refreshments to that area.

Brag a little

Dedication time is a good time for reminiscing, so find a speaker who can bring the library's history to life. When, why, and how was the library begun? By whom? What was its original location? How many other buildings has it been housed in? How many volumes were in the original collection? While accuracy is important, those who want a mere listing of facts can find it elsewhere—probably in the library's reference collection. Instead, encourage the speaker to tell anecdotes and to recall special hurdles and colorful people who helped the library overcome them.

Next, focus on the present: Why was the present construction necessary? How was the move accomplished? What will the new location mean to library services? What will the library offer now that it could not before the move?

Then, look to the future: How many volumes can this building hold at capacity and how long will it take to reach that point? What new services might be introduced? Where is technology going and how will it affect this library?

A dedication ceremony is also a time to express thankfulness and to honor those who have helped make the library what it is today. Recognize each contributor in some way, no matter how small an individual donation of time, money, or expertise might have been. But do not feel obligated to read aloud all 547 names of those who have donated five dollars; instead, list contributors in the program and publicly thank them en masse during the ceremony. While donors of large sums often get the most attention, organizers should take care to show that each donor is important.

Some communities expect the ceremony to include an offering of thanks to God for the new library. A musical tribute is one of many ways for doing so.

A ribbon-cutting is a natural part of dedication day. When more than one person should receive the honor of cutting the ribbon, give each honoree a pair of scissors and have everyone cut simultaneously. Or use several ribbons, with each honored guest cutting one.

To ensure that the media gets good photos of the library, give ribbon cutters a tip from Otis Bowen, U.S. Secretary of Health and Human Services. Before cutting the ribbon in front of Bethel College's new Otis and Elizabeth Bowen Library, he quickly ducked under the ribbon and turned to face the audience, remarking, "If there's one thing I've learned from all my years in public office, it's never to turn my back to the cameras."

Visitors must have an opportunity to see the new facility, which, after all, is the whole reason for the gathering. Even patrons who have frequented the new building might like a tour; preoccupied on previous visits, they may never have explored the library's new home. Tours may be self-conducted or led by a staffer.

Conclude any dedication ceremony with an invitation to all those present to use their new library. If people go away feeling good about the dedication, they are likely to become library users—and maybe supporters.

Dennis C. Tucker, Reference and Periodicals Librarian at Mishawaka-Penn Public Library, Mishawaka, Indiana, is the author of From Here to There: Moving a Library _(Wyndham Hall, 1987), and directed Bethel College Library from 1983 to 1987._

The Proper Dedication Day

ANNE M. TURNER and *MARGARET PELIKAN*

(From *American Libraries*, April 1990. Copyright 1990 by ALA. Reprinted with permission.)

First things first. The dedication ceremony for the new building is at 10 a.m. this morning, and we know that you and the staff have been up all night trying to get the children's picture books to fit into that darling little nook the architect insisted upon. Not to mention cleaning up the shambles in Tech Services.

Nevertheless, go home, take a bath, put on your best drop-dead outfit, and start smiling. This is it, kid. You did it. And for the rest of the day, try to remember some advice for excruciatingly correct behavior from two of us who have been there.

Suitable footwear and face

Do *not* wear open-toed shoes. The new landscaping may be lovely, but you know as well as we do that the sprinkler system test went badly yesterday, and nothing is more uncomfortable than gooshy feet when you are trying to smile.

A blank expression, varied occasionally by a polite smile, is the correct one while listening to the high school band play "Marian the Librarian" in the staff's honor.

The same response is also correct while listening to the mayor explain how he/she has "always loved libraries."

Avoid snarling when you overhear the board chair telling local reporters how hard he/she personally worked to get the building built.

A wise director will carefully rehearse her response prior to meeting the community member who advocated the operating budget be cut by $100,000 because the new building was going to be so much more "efficient."

A wise director will also strongly brief her staff—particularly that reference librarian who prides herself on "telling it like it is"—on what they should say about the new building: They *love* it; they are individually and collectively *thrilled* at the opportunities it will provide for better service. The air conditioning system isn't working and the temperature is 105? Later. Make dire threats, if necessary, or bribe them.

Who said they're bygones?

Relations with the project architect are particularly difficult to manage during launch day. We realize that the two of you were last on friendly terms 18 months ago when the construction contract was signed. Your task now is to maintain a frosty smile while *not* letting bygones be bygones. After all, you know as well as he does that the west slope is going to erode, and that the sightlines from the circ desk are abysmal.

But the clown may well win an architectural award for the library building. You and he and the Main Reading Room are going to be photographed from now until eternity. Your task is therefore to convey the impression, no doubt correct, that the truly innovative aspects of the design flowed from your suggestions, whereas the problems that any fool can easily identify were caused by his failure to listen. You must, however do this without actually saying so.

Coddle that contractor

Your demeanor towards the construction contractor, on the other hand, *must* be cordial, even if you technically aren't speaking to him either. The reason is that the building is still under warranty. For the moment, problems will be more easily solved if you are on speaking terms. Not to worry . . . you'll see him in court later.

In your dedication remarks from the podium, be brief. No one else will be, but a good example never hurts. On the one hand this is not a time for whining—no one but you and the staff cares how much you have all suffered in the old building. On the other, it also isn't a moment for one of those awful Academy Award speeches ("I'd like to thank my mother, my father, the city purchasing agent . . ."). Write all those people personal notes tomorrow.

Instead, try a little spontaneity. Something like, "I'm not going to tell you how much I really hate this building. Just kidding, heh, heh. We will try to use it wisely and well. Thank you, taxpayers, very much!"

And remember one thing: you, the staff, all your spouses, and every visiting librarian who has ever built a building know what you have gone through to get this one open. Your reward will be in heaven. We promise.

Visiting others' kickoffs

You may ask gently what the square-footage cost of the new building was, but you may *not* ask what her predecessor predicted it would be back in 1955, when she/he first declared the new building was crucial to continued service.

Restrain any tactless urge to use words or phrases such as "finally" or "at last"—particularly in the exclamatory mode—when congratulating the director on getting the damn thing open.

It is also tactless to observe that the collection seems crowded for a brand-new building. The director already knows the sacrifices in square footage that were made to achieve the avant garde diagonal upward thrust of the stairwell design, and doesn't need you to rub it in.

Overt displays of jealousy should be avoided at all costs. It is okay to go back to your own library and grouch to your secretary about the waste of building such a monument for a community as tacky as Smithville. While at the site, however, try to maintain a manner of gracious patronage.

Do *not* comment on the aforementioned abysmal sightlines from the circ desk. If absolutely necessary you may console yourself by lingering ostentatiously in that stupid children's nook, wearing an expression of bemused curiosity.

It is also okay to get your own board chair, mayor, or other holder of purse strings to come with you to the dedication. Then while the band is playing "Marian the Librarian," you whisper something along the lines of "Well, I always thought we in Jonesville had it all over Smithville, but this is really something, isn't it?" This ploy works even better if you can get a reporter (preferably a sportswriter) from your own local paper to come.

And remember: Do not wear open-toed shoes.

Anne M. Turner is the director of the Santa Cruz (California) City/County Library System. Margaret Pelikan is the director of the Harrison Memorial Library in Carmel-by-the-Sea. Turner opened a new branch in 1985 and Pelikan a renovated building in 1989. They attended each other's dedication ceremonies, and both behaved beautifully.

6

The Honeymoon's Over

🏛 ***Don't pay retainer fees until you and your board are satisfied.***

When the architect's office considers a contractor's work to be complete, they will forward to you the approved request for payment, which includes the final retainer fee. Once this is paid, they are gone. This is your last chance, so if you aren't satisfied, speak now or forever hold your peace. Is the heat and air conditioning properly balanced? Does the carpet have fraying edges? Has the paint been touched up?

Most contracts stipulate that all workmanship and materials are warranted for one year after completion, but this is mainly intended to protect you when things break down after minimal use. Things that are wrong now should be fixed now. It's a lot easier to get someone to work on a problem while you still hold some of their money. Try to get as many of the bugs worked out as possible before you pay.

🏛 ***Keep all your project-related files easily accessible for two years.***

During punch listing, and during the warranty period, you'll want to be able to get to all your files readily. Also, when the auditor comes to call, all those files will be needed. Put them into a cardboard box or two and keep them handy.

Keep meticulous track of the punch lists.

The punch list is the contractor's list of all the piddly little details that need to be finished or corrected before the job is considered to be complete. Even the best contractors can become dilatory about this part of the project. They have to track down subcontractors (some of whom may have gone out of business by now) and schedule them to come to your building for a job that may only take half an hour to do. It's hard for them to find time for this sort of thing. Nevertheless, this is part of their contract, and it's up to you to make sure they don't forget about it. Keep a copy of the list and check off each item as it's completed. Don't let any be missed. The architect won't want to make more than one trip to your site to check, so be sure that everything is done before then.

 Reevaluate your library and personnel policies.

For a long time you've been preoccupied with getting a building built. Chances are that during this period your personnel manuals have gone out of date. People's jobs have changed, sometimes drastically. You may have new positions. The job classification system may no longer be big enough or flexible enough for your new needs.

If you've never had a meeting room before, you'll need to draft a meeting room policy. You may not have any procedures in place for library tours, and there are going to be plenty of them. Your selection and collection development policies were designed for a smaller collection.

All in all, there are probably half a dozen policies and procedures that will need to be rewritten. And how long has it been since you updated the long-range plan?

 Expect a rash of minor personnel problems.

No one knows why, exactly, but virtually every library experiences an outbreak of severe whining once the building is finished. We were all good little soldiers for so long. We endured noise, dust, heat, cold, and gloom of night with a smile on our lips and a song in our hearts. Now, despite the spiffy new surroundings, it's back to business as usual. At the very least, there's a psychological letdown. Nothing exciting is happening any more. There are just ornery patrons and grouchy coworkers. Personality clashes that have slumbered awaken again. Departmental rivalries resurface.

For months we were able to blame everything that went wrong on the architect or the contractor. Now we're left with only one another to pick on.

Maybe there really isn't any more complaining than usual. Maybe we were just too preoccupied to pay any attention before. At any rate, your staff is not especially wayward. It happens to us all. It will pass.

🏛 *Try not to plan any new projects for at least six months or a year. Give everyone a chance to settle in.*

Many librarians look toward the end of a building project with some trepidation. With no construction crises to handle, what will you do all day? Some of us are tempted to fill the expected vacuum with major projects: A new YA program, a volunteer project for latchkey kids, a senior citizens' story hour. After all, you have this wonderful new facility, and you'll want to use it right away.

That's fine. But don't dive into a new project before you have time to catch your breath from this one. Give your staff time to get acclimated to their new surroundings. Give yourself time to investigate to see what projects are needed. Give your budget time to reflect new utility and maintenance costs.

Don't think you'll be twiddling your thumbs during this period, either. There will be plenty to keep you occupied. The punch list process will take at least six months. It will take all winter to get the heating adjusted properly. By that time you'll have to start fiddling with the air conditioning. All of those outdated policies and procedures need to be rewritten. And you want to get that four hours of raw videotape edited into a coherent presentation.

🏛 *Get a statement of values for your property and use it to select the proper insurance coverage.*

During construction you carried builder's risk insurance. That policy should now be canceled and new coverage purchased. At this point, many libraries solicit quotations from selected carriers. So you have a dozen or so investigators wandering over the building, or calling you and your clerk-treasurer to ask questions. Some want to know how much you paid for the addition. Some ask for square footage figures. Some want to know the construction materials. No two seem to ask the same set of questions. So when the quotes come in, they range from $3,500 a year to $16,000. How do you know what you really need?

It is helpful to have a statement of values prepared by an independent appraiser. Your current insurance agent should be able to recommend one, or you can check with local schools and businesses, especially those that have built or remodeled recently. The statement of values can be distributed to all of the insurance carriers from whom you want quotes. Then they will all be working from the same baseline. Extras can be quoted separately. You won't be able to get a statement of values until the project is virtually complete, because the appraiser will want to see the furnishings and equipment in place. So don't forget to renew your current coverage with a reasonable upgrade in the meantime.

Start a notebook of items to include in the next building project.

When you and your staff planned this building, you forgot something, probably several things. When the architects designed it, they made a mistake here or there. The contractors who built it had occasional mix-ups. The new "smart" HVAC system is dependent on poorly placed thermostats, so some areas roast while others freeze. New computer terminals are placed in areas with bad glare from overhead lights. The staff lounge door, refrigerator, and restroom are all huddled in one end of the room, creating major traffic jams every noon. It won't take long for you to discover those things that should be remedied when the next remodeling is done.

Legislation affecting public buildings changes rapidly. The passage of the Americans with Disabilities Act (ADA) in 1991 may have rendered many new buildings obsolete already. I say "may" because, as of this writing, no one is sure exactly what structural accommodations are going to be needed, by whom or when.

The introduction of new technologies will make demands upon your building as well. Twenty years ago no library needed video shelving. Our collections will change as our patrons' needs change, and our buildings will have to change too.

When you began your building project, you probably had no experience with architects, designers, or contractors. If you had known then what you know now, you might have approached the design phase with a different set of requirements. Now is the time to start logging these requirements for the next time. Some day, five or fifty years from now, someone will say, "This library needs to be re-done." Your ideas, culled from experience, will be useful to whoever is in charge of that project, even if you have long since shuffled off to that great reading room in the sky. Leave behind a record of concerns and ideas for that person to consider, just as you leave behind the as-built drawings. After all, providing information is your job.

Selected Bibliography

Some of the following books were useful to me in preparing for my building project. Others did not come out until the project was finished and I was working on this book, but they certainly *would* have been useful to me!

Christensen, John O. *Planning Library Buildings in the 1980s: A Selective Bibliography.* Monticello, Ill.: Vance Bibliographies, 1989.

Though a bit old, this bibliography provided some useful readings to get me going.

Design & Construction Administration for New & Remodeled Libraries. Savannah, Ga.: Fitzgerald Foundation/Maddox & Associates, P.C., 1988.

This manual was provided at a PLA/SMLS preconference in 1988. It takes you through the entire process, step by step, showing what gets done and whose responsibility it is. It made a good security blanket for me to carry on my two-year odyssey.

Fraley, Ruth A., and Carol L. Anderson. *Library Space Planning: A How-to-Do-It Manual for Assessing, Allocating & Reorganizing Collections, Resources & Facilities.* New York: Neal-Schuman, 1990.

Makes recommendations for assessing the library's space requirements in order to meet both present and future needs, including setting priorities. Also includes information on budget management, PR, and coordinating the move into a new building.

Hart, Thomas L. *Creative Ideas for Library Media Center Facilities.* Englewood, Colo.: Libraries Unlimited, 1990.

An idea book for school librarians, it includes a lot of useful suggestions for planning light and inviting areas for children. It also has a number of nifty ideas for cozy nooks and play structures, if you have the room.

Holt, Raymond M. *Planning Library Buildings & Facilities (From Concept to Completion).* Metuchen, N.J.: Scarecrow Press, 1989.

Step-by-step description of the planning process, including guidelines for determining space requirements.

Lushington, Nolan A., and James M. Kusack. *Design & Evaluation of Public Library Buildings.* Hamden, Conn.: Shoe String Press, 1991.
Outlines a process for planning a building that uses input from output measures for public libraries. Builds on themes first presented in Lushington's earlier book, below.

Lushington, Nolan A., and Willis N. Mills, Jr. *Libraries Designed for Users: A Planning Handbook.* Hamden, Conn.: Library Professional Publications/Shoe String Press, 1980.
This landmark book promulgates the theory that the needs of the user, not the warehousing of books or the convenience of the staff, should dictate design.

Manley, Will. *Unintellectual Freedoms: Opinions of a Public Librarian.* Jefferson, N.C.: McFarland, 1991.
This collection of Manley's "Facing the Public" columns includes some comments on building and a lot of irreverent musings on the profession in general. Keep it on your night stand and laugh yourself to sleep.

Oehlerts, Donald E. *Books & Blueprints: Building America's Public Libraries.* Westport, Conn.: Greenwood Press, 1991.
A historical overview of how public libraries were designed from 1850 to 1989, giving major metropolitan facilities as examples. Good background in the evolution of library design.

Sannwald, William W., and Robert S. Smith, eds. *Checklist of Library Building Design Considerations.* Chicago: American Library Association, 1991.
A master list of hundreds of memory-prodding questions to ask yourself during the design phase. It should help keep you from forgetting some vital point.

Smith, Lester K., ed. *Planning Library Buildings: From Decision to Design.* Chicago: Library Administration and Management Association/American Library Association, 1986.
Collected papers from an ALA preconference in 1984. Not as useful as *Design & Construction,* mentioned above, but has some thought-provoking information in it.

Stephenson, Mary S. *Planning Library Facilities: A Selected Annotated Bibliography.* Metuchen, N.J.: Scarecrow Press, 1990.
Like the Christensen bibliography, mentioned above, this work gets you into a research mood.

Floor Plans and Elevations

A library building project may be a large undertaking or a relatively moderate one for all parties involved—the library staff, the architects, the city and county officials, and so on. A project's total cost may range from hundreds of thousands of dollars to millions. The following section contains floor plans and elevations for a variety of remodeled libraries, both large and small undertakings. The idea is to give you options and inspiration for your own library building project. You may find that some of the following plans and layouts work for your library. You may like one of the following plans so much that you will want to contact the architect who did the work to talk about your own project. That is certainly an option for you because all of this information has been provided on a contents sheet, preceding each group of floor plans, with credits to the various architectural firms who were kind enough to provide usable drawings. All firms went out of their way to be helpful, which the author appreciates very much.

A wide variety of resources are available for libraries embarking on a building program. *Library Journal*'s annual Architectural Issue comes out every December. It lists buildings currently under construction and recently finished, providing information about the size and costs of each, along with the architect's name and address, as well as information about how the projects were funded. The photographs alone are enough to revive one's flagging enthusiasm. Keep this issue handy.

The Library Administration & Management Association (LAMA) puts out the *Library Buildings Consultants List*, which provides information about consultants who specialize in this area. Included are the number of years the consultant has been in business; the number of projects the consultant has completed; the consultant's five most recent projects; and areas of expertise and details on fees, time, and geographic limitations, if any. If you decide to use this list, be aware that all the consultants included have provided their own information and paid LAMA a $50 fee to be listed. Be sure to check their references before you sign on the dotted line.

Many state libraries keep a current list of consultants and architects who specialize in building projects. Some provide their own consultants to assist librarians in planning and hiring architects. In states that do not provide such services, try calling your state association and asking if they have such information. Even if they don't, they can probably give you the names and numbers of people around your state who have done building projects recently.

Most of the professional journals do occasional articles on buildings. Keep an eye on *Library Literature*, and build your own file of relevant articles for future reference. The ALA and PLA conferences often have programs on building projects, and these are also wonderful places to meet others who are involved in such projects. People who have already done what you want to do are the best sources of information. Find as many as you can and ask them what they did, who helped them do it, and what they would do differently if they had the chance.

Good luck!

Artist's Rendition, the new Denver Central Library. (Drawing by Michael Graves, FAIA.)

Denver Central Library

Denver, Colorado

Klipp Colussy Jenks DuBois, Architects, P.C., and Michael Graves, Architect.

Page 76: Photograph of model, Denver Central Library. (Photograph © 1993, Thorney Lieberman.)

Page 77: Level 1, Schematic Design, Denver Central Library

Page 78: Level 2, Schematic Design, Denver Central Library

Page 79: Level 3, Schematic Design, Denver Central Library

Page 80: Level 4, Schematic Design, Denver Central Library

Page 81: Level 5, Schematic Design, Denver Central Library

Page 82: Level 6, Schematic Design, Denver Central Library

Page 83: Level 7, Schematic Design, Denver Central Library

Page 84: Basement Level 1, Schematic Design, Denver Central Library

Page 85: Basement Level 2, Schematic Design, Denver Central Library

The City and County of Denver is calling its renovation of the Central Library downtown a *new* library incorporating the current library. One goal of the expansion is to preserve the historic Burnham Hoyt building, and the city found the right architects to do just that. "We envision the expanded Denver Central Library as one of Denver's most important civic structures of the decade, reflecting the activities and architecture of its community. Our design preserves the integrity of the Hoyt building," according to Klipp Colussy Jenks DuBois, Architects, P.C., of Denver. "We chose different, but complementary exterior materials for the addition to maintain the color, texture, and proportions of Hoyt's composition. Further, by breaking the large mass into smaller parts, the scale is more sympathetic to that of the existing building." Ground was broken for the new library in April 1993 and is scheduled for completion in spring 1995. In addition to being able to provide the latest technology to its patrons, the new Denver Central Library will have an

increased staff, better materials and resources, and more space—
much more space, as evidenced in the floor plans that follow. This
is truly an amazing project!

Plans were submitted for this publication by Klipp Colossy
Jenks DuBois, Architects, P.C. (1200 Seventeenth Street, Suite
1100, Denver, Colorado 80202) for the Denver Central Library.

Project Data: Michael Graves, FAIA, and Klipp Colussy Jenks
DuBois, Architects, P.C.; approximately 525,000 square feet; cost:
$65 million; City and County of Denver.

*Photograph of model, Denver Central Library. (Photograph © 1993,
Thorney Lieberman.)*

Level 1, Schematic Design, Denver Central Library

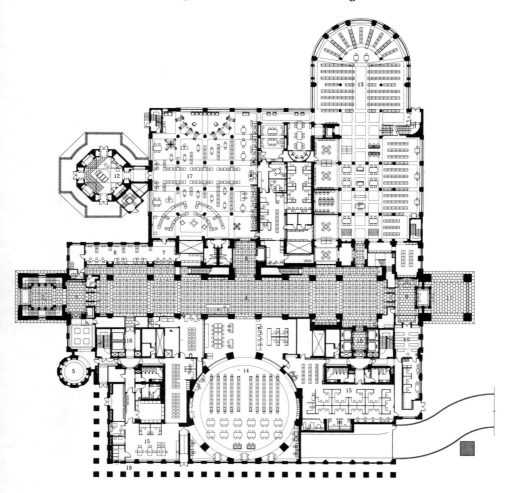

LEVEL 1

1. ACOMA PLAZA
2. WEST TOWER ENTRANCE
3. WEST LOBBY
4. GREAT HALL
5. LIBRARY STORE
6. REGISTRATION/CHECKOUT
7. CHILDREN'S CHECKOUT
8. CHILDREN'S ENTRY HALL
9. EAST LOBBY
10. ORIENTATION

11. EAST TOWER ENTRANCE
12. CHILDREN'S PAVILION
13. ADULT FICTION COLLECTION
14. REFERENCE READING ROOM
15. WORKROOM
16. SERVICE ELEVATOR
17. CHILDREN'S LIBRARY
18. ELEVATOR LOBBY
19. BOOK DROP

Klipp Colussy Jenks DuBois, Architects, P.C., and Michael Graves, Architect

Level 2, Schematic Design, Denver Central Library

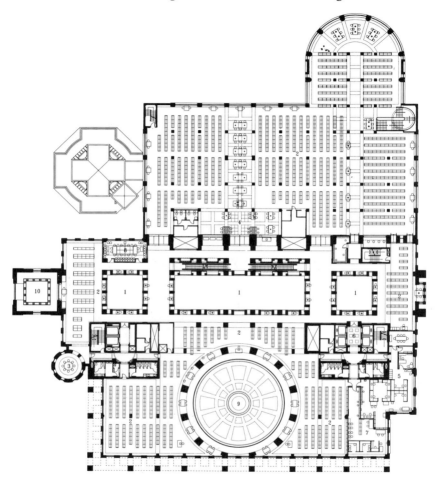

LEVEL 2

1. OPEN TO GREAT HALL BELOW
2. NON-FICTION COLLECTION
3. READING ROOM
4. READING AREA
5. COLLECTION DEVELOPMENT
6. ELEVATOR LOBBY
7. WORKROOM
8. MEETING ROOM
9. OPEN TO REFERENCE READING ROOM
   BELOW
10. OPEN TO WEST ENTRANCE BELOW

Klipp Colussy Jenks DuBois, Architects, P.C., and Michael Graves, Architect

Level 3, Schematic Design, Denver Central Library

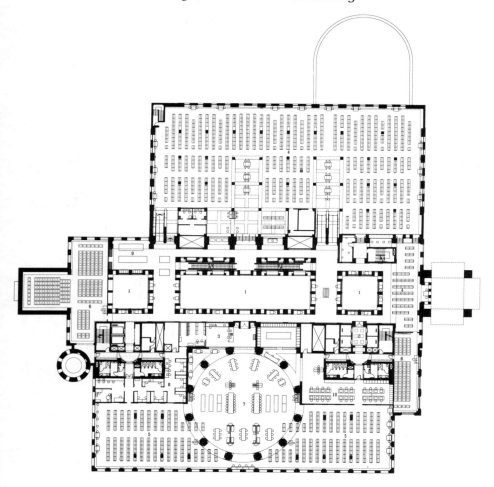

LEVEL 3

1. OPEN TO GREAT HALL BELOW
2. ELEVATOR LOBBY
3. SERVICE DESK
4. NON-FICTION COLLECTION
5. MAGAZINE COLLECTION
6. CLOSED STACKS
7. MAGAZINE READING ROOM
8. WORKROOM
9. FILES
10. MICROFORM

Klipp Colussy Jenks DuBois, Architects, P.C., and Michael Graves, Architect

Level 4, Schematic Design, Denver Central Library

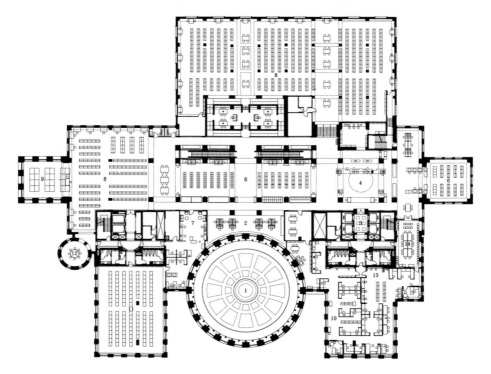

LEVEL 4

1. OPEN TO MAGAZINE ROOM BELOW
2. CD-ROM
3. ELEVATOR LOBBY
4. SERVICE DESK
5. CATALOGUES
6. PATENT COLLECTION
7. DOCUMENT DELIVERY
   MICROFORM
8. GOVERNMENT PUBLICATIONS/
   BUSINESS
9. MAPS
10. INTERLIBRARY LOAN
11. CLOSED STACKS
12. READING ROOM
13. WORKROOM
14. MEETING ROOM

Klipp Colussy Jenks DuBois, Architects, P.C., and Michael Graves, Architect

Level 5, Schematic Design, Denver Central Library

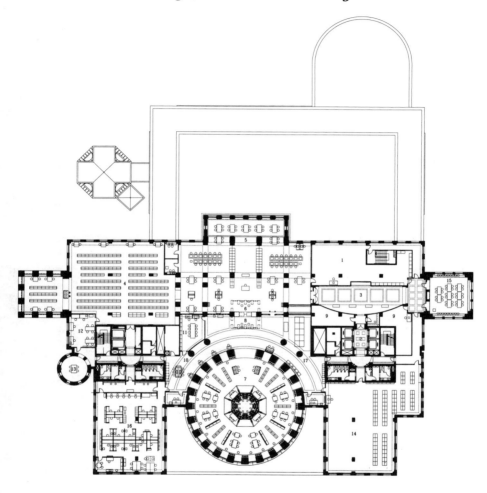

LEVEL 5

1. FILES AND CLOSED STACKS
2. ELEVATOR LOBBY
3. GALLERY
4. GENEALOGY STACKS
5. GENEALOGY READING ROOM
6. GENEALOGY SERVICE DESK
7. WESTERN HISTORY READING ROOM
8. WESTERN HISTORY SERVICE DESK
9. ART STORAGE

10. PHOTO AUTOMATION
11. MANUSCRIPTS READING ROOM
12. WORKROOM
13. STAFF PROJECTS ROOM
14. FILES AND CLOSED STACKS
15. MEETING ROOM
16. WORKROOM
17. MAPS

Klipp Colussy Jenks DuBois, Architects, P.C., and Michael Graves, Architect

Level 6, Schematic Design, Denver Central Library

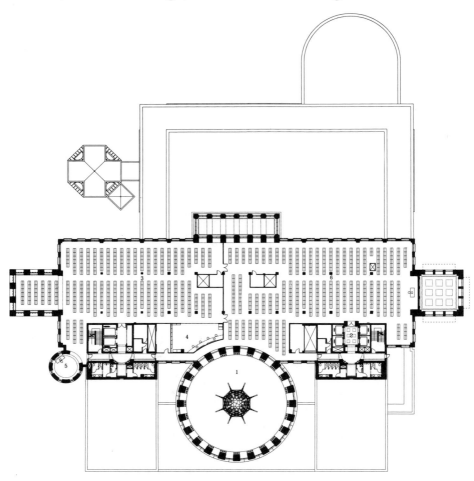

LEVEL 6

1. OPEN TO BELOW
2. ELEVATOR LOBBY
3. WESTERN HISTORY CLOSED STACKS
4. MANUSCRIPT PROCESSING
5. WORKROOM
6. CLOSED STACKS

Klipp Colussy Jenks DuBois, Architects, P.C., and Michael Graves, Architect

Level 7, Schematic Design, Denver Central Library

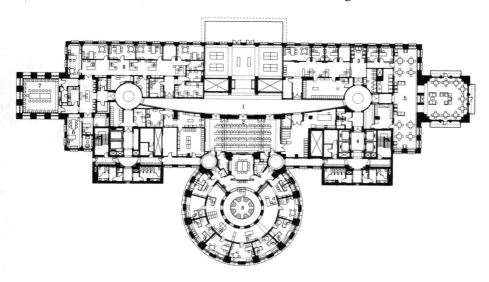

LEVEL 7

1. GALLERY
2. TRAINING ROOM
3. HUMAN RESOURCES
4. ELEVATOR LOBBY
5. STAFF LOUNGE
6. CITY LIBRARY
7. MEETING ROOM
8. ADMINISTRATIVE OFFICES

Klipp Colussy Jenks DuBois, Architects, P.C., and Michael Graves, Architect

Basement Level 1, Schematic Design, Denver Central Library

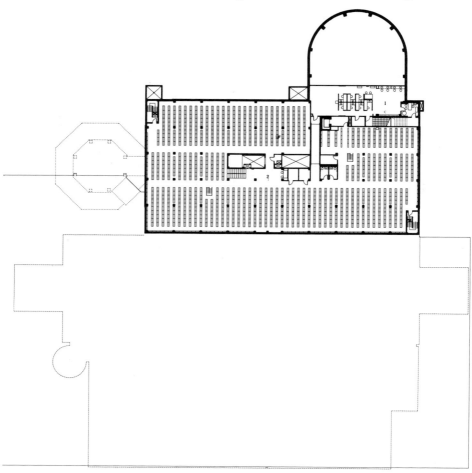

BASEMENT LEVEL 1

1. WORKROOM
2. CLOSED STACKS

Klipp Colussy Jenks DuBois, Architects, P.C., and Michael Graves, Architect

Basement Level 2, Schematic Design, Denver Central Library

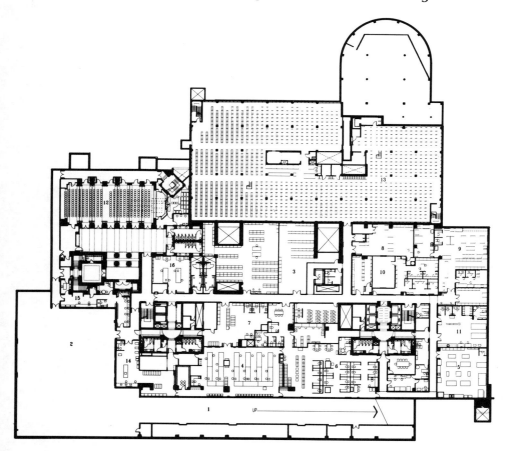

BASEMENT LEVEL 2

1. SERVICE RAMP
2. LOADING DOCK
3. STORAGE
4. PROCESSING
5. CONSERVATION AND
   PRESERVATION
6. CATALOGUING
7. ACQUISITIONS
8. CARPENTRY SHOP
9. PRINT SHOP
10. COMPUTER ROOM
11. PUBLICATIONS STUDIO
12. MULTI-PURPOSE ROOM
13. CLOSED STACKS
14. MAIL ROOM
15. SECURITY
16. MOBILE SERVICES

Klipp Colussy Jenks DuBois, Architects, P.C., and Michael Graves, Architect

Boulder Public Library

Boulder, Colorado

Midyette, Seieroe, Architects

Let there be light! In December 1993, the newly renovated Boulder Public Library was selected to appear on the cover of *Library Journal*. The modernness of the structure is reflected not only from a physical standpoint, but also from a functional perspective. The architects took into consideration the efficient use of solar energy for heating and lighting. To reduce annual electrical consumption and peak demand charges, the daylighting system was designed to work on clear, partly cloudy, and overcast days. The use of natural light inside the library was taken advantage of wherever possible. Daylight is reflected off the light-colored roofs, light shelves, and interior ledges to provide diffused natural lighting throughout the library. This indirect daylight results in a softly glowing interior that permits outward views to trees, clouds, and sky without glare. It's a design that has gone over very well with the environmentally conscious residents of Boulder, Colorado.

Plans were submitted for this publication by Midyette, Seieroe, Architects (3300 28th Street, Suite 200, Boulder, Colorado 80301) for the Boulder Public Library.

Conceptual Site and Landscape Plan, Boulder Public Library

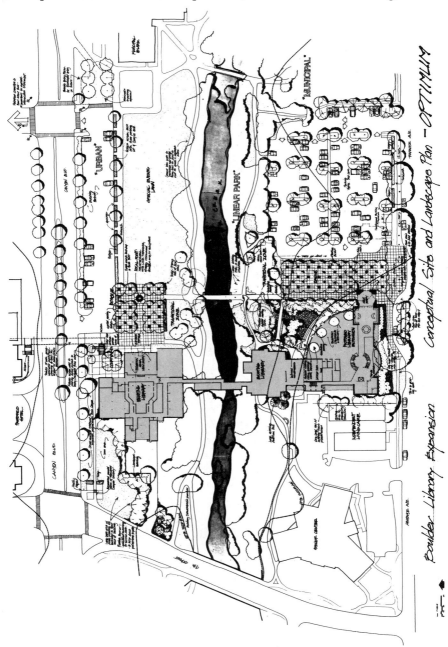

Midyette, Seieroe, Architects

Elevation, Boulder Public Library

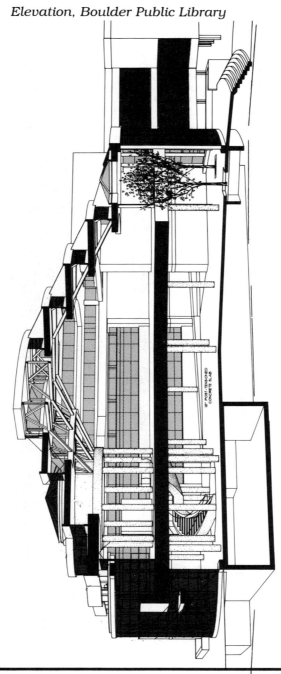

Midyette, Seieroe, Architects

Elevation, Building Section AA, Boulder Public Library

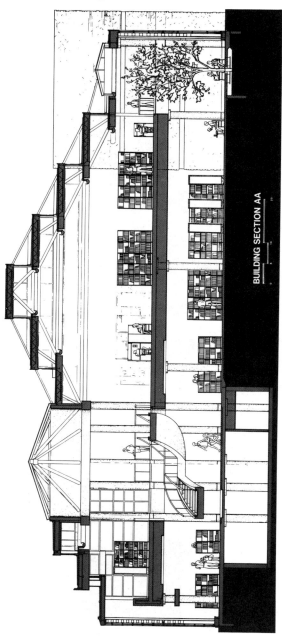

Midyette, Seieroe, Architects

Additional Site Plan, Boulder Public Library

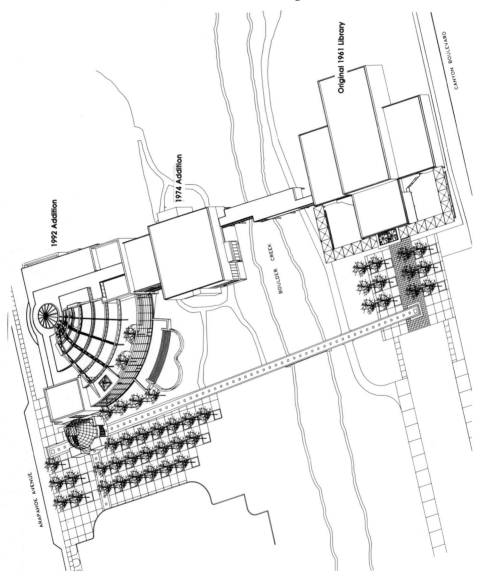

Midyette, Seieroe, Architects

Original 1961 First Level Floor Plan, Boulder Public Library

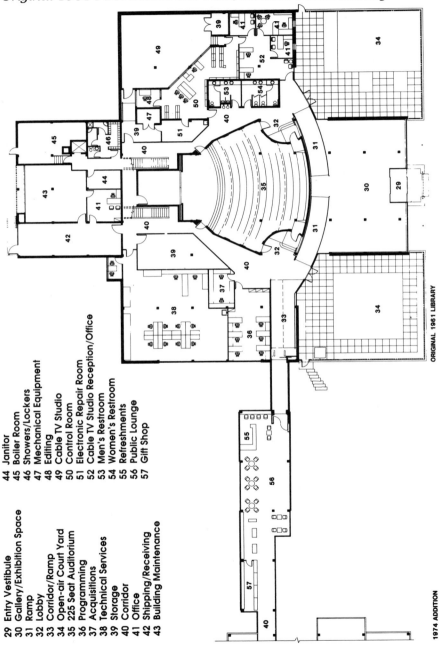

ORIGINAL 1961 LIBRARY

1974 ADDITION

29 Entry Vestibule
30 Gallery/Exhibition Space
31 Ramp
32 Lobby
33 Corridor/Ramp
34 Open-air Court Yard
35 225 Seat Auditorium
36 Programming
37 Acquisitions
38 Technical Services
39 Storage
40 Corridor
41 Office
42 Shipping/Receiving
43 Building Maintenance

44 Janitor
45 Boiler Room
46 Showers/Lockers
47 Mechanical Equipment
48 Editing
49 Cable TV Studio
50 Control Room
51 Electronic Repair Room
52 Cable TV Studio Reception/Office
53 Men's Restroom
54 Women's Restroom
55 Refreshments
56 Public Lounge
57 Gift Shop

Midyette, Seieroe, Architects

1974 and 1992 Additions, First Floor Plan, Boulder Public Library

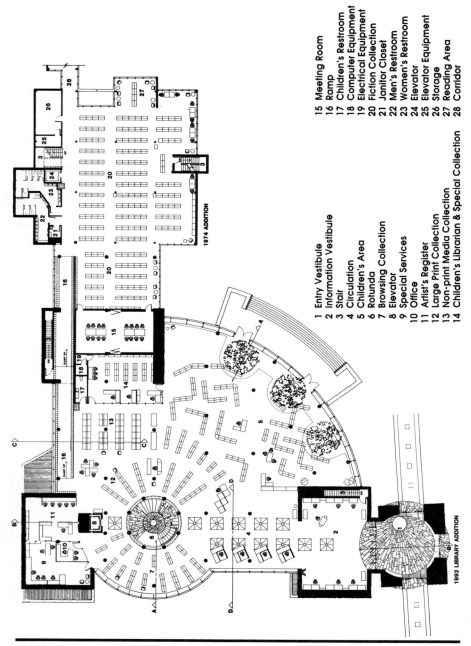

1 Entry Vestibule
2 Information Vestibule
3 Stair
4 Circulation
5 Children's Area
6 Rotunda
7 Browsing Collection
8 Elevator
9 Special Services
10 Office
11 Artist's Register
12 Large Print Collection
13 Non-print Media Collection
14 Children's Librarian & Special Collection

15 Meeting Room
16 Ramp
17 Children's Restroom
18 Computer Equipment
19 Electrical Equipment
20 Fiction Collection
21 Janitor Closet
22 Men's Restroom
23 Women's Restroom
24 Elevator
25 Elevator Equipment
26 Storage
27 Reading Area
28 Corridor

Midyette, Seieroe, Architects

1974 and 1992 Additions, Second Level Floor Plan, Boulder Public Library

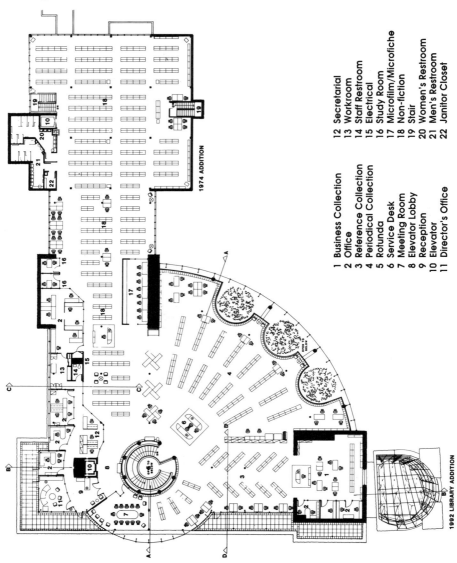

1   Business Collection
2   Office
3   Reference Collection
4   Periodical Collection
5   Rotunda
6   Service Desk
7   Meeting Room
8   Elevator Lobby
9   Reception
10   Elevator
11   Director's Office

12   Secretarial
13   Workroom
14   Staff Restroom
15   Electrical
16   Study Room
17   Microfilm/Microfiche
18   Non-fiction
19   Stair
20   Women's Restroom
21   Men's Restroom
22   Janitor Closet

1974 ADDITION

1992 LIBRARY ADDITION

1961 Second Level Floor Plan/Roof Plan, Boulder Public Library

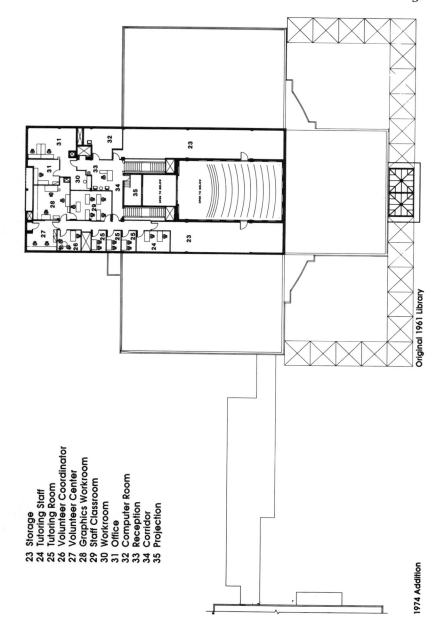

23 Storage
24 Tutoring Staff
25 Tutoring Room
26 Volunteer Coordinator
27 Volunteer Center
28 Graphics Workroom
29 Staff Classroom
30 Workroom
31 Office
32 Computer Room
33 Reception
34 Corridor
35 Projection

1974 Addition

Original 1961 Library

Midyette, Seieroe, Architects

Van Wylen Library

Hope College, Holland, Michigan

Shepley Bulfinch Richardson and Abbott, Architects

In 1989, the American Institute of Architects and the American Library Association awarded their Library Buildings Award to the Van Wylen Library at Hope College in Holland, Michigan. It was designed by Shepley Bulfinch Richardson and Abbott (40 Broad Street, Boston, Massachusetts 02109).

Ground Floor, Hope College, Holland, Michigan

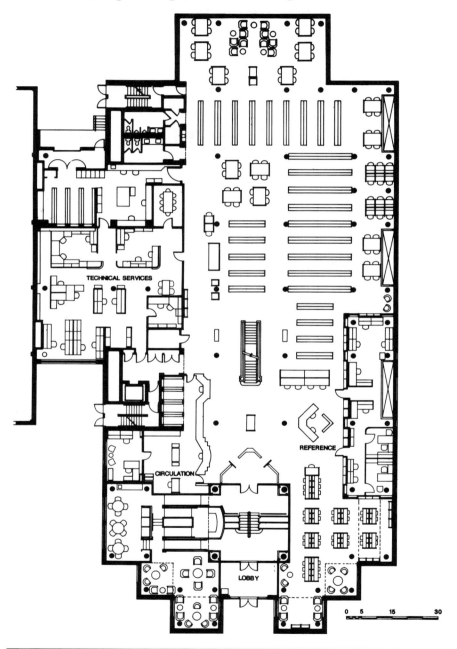

Shepley Bulfinch Richardson and Abbott, Architects

Second Floor, Hope College, Holland, Michigan

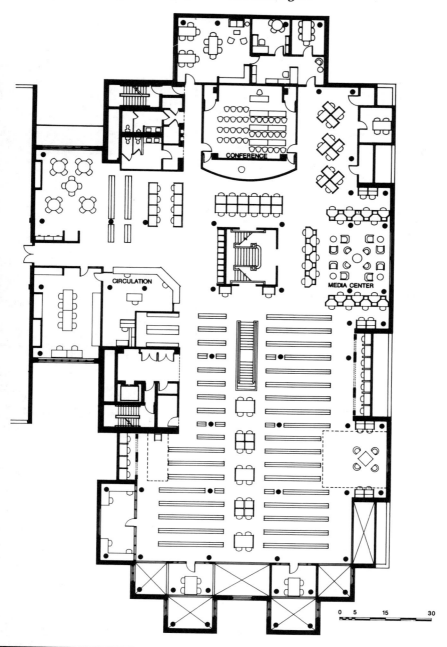

Shepley Bulfinch Richardson and Abbott, Architects

Third Floor, Hope College, Holland, Michigan

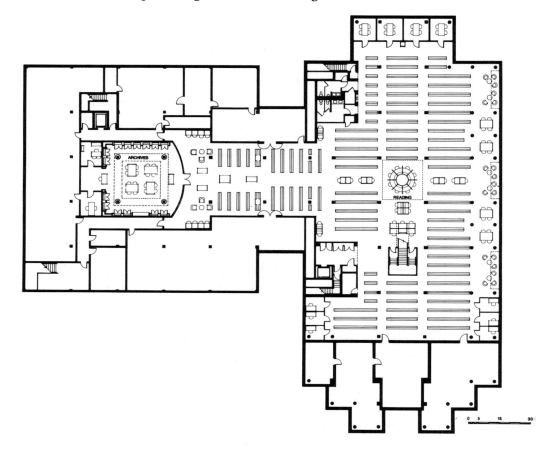

Shepley Bulfinch Richardson and Abbott, Architects

Fourth Floor, Hope College, Holland, Michigan

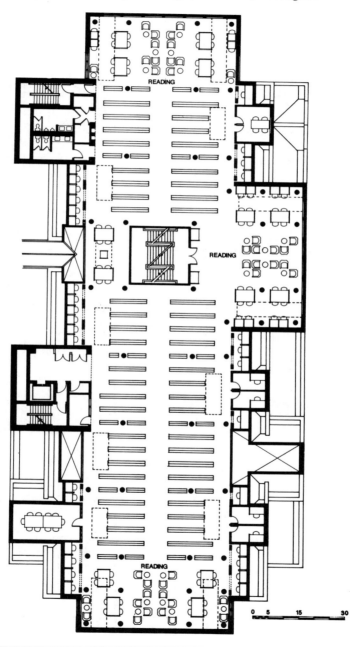

Shepley Bulfinch Richardson and Abbott, Architects

Fifth Floor, Hope College, Holland, Michigan

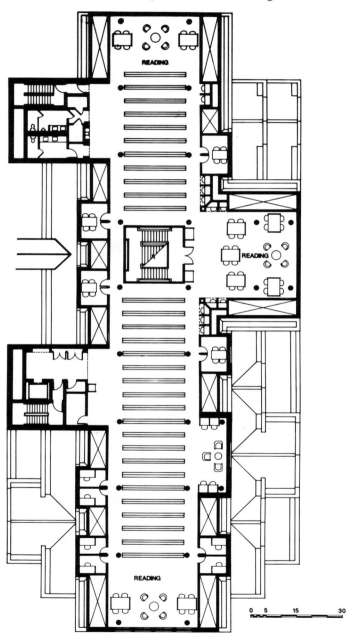

Shepley Bulfinch Richardson and Abbott, Architects

East Palestine Memorial Library
East Palestine, Ohio
Beck and Tabeling Architects, Inc.

Page 104: Pre-Remodeling First Floor Plan, East Palestine Memorial Library

Page 105: Remodeled First Floor Plan, East Palestine Memorial Library

Drawings for the East Palestine Memorial Library, a public library in East Palestine, Ohio, were submitted by Beck and Tabeling Architects, Inc., Akron, Ohio.

103

Pre-Remodeling First Floor Plan, East Palestine Memorial Library

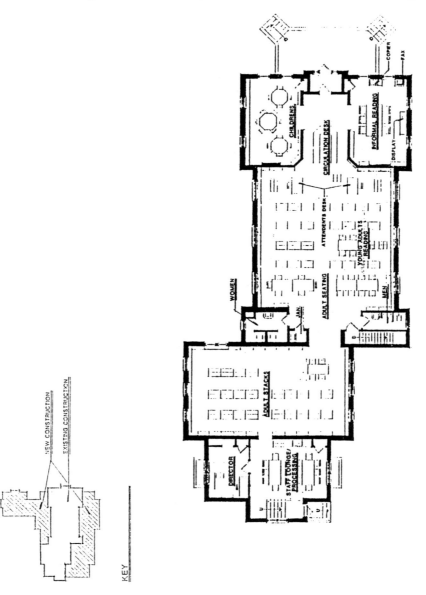

Remodeled First Floor Plan, East Palestine Memorial Library

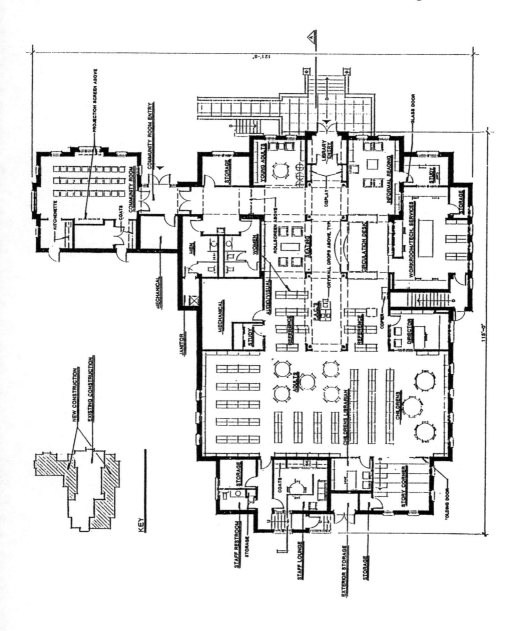

Beck and Tabeling Architects, Inc.

Cerritos Public Library

Cerritos, California

Charles Walton Associates

Page 108: First Floor Plan, Cerritos Public Library

Page 109: Second Floor/Mezzanine Plan, Cerritos Public Library

Plans for the Cerritos Public Library expansion were submitted by Charles Walton Associates, AIA, Inc. (320 Arden Avenue, Suite 210, Glendale, California 91203).

First Floor Plan, Cerritos Public Library

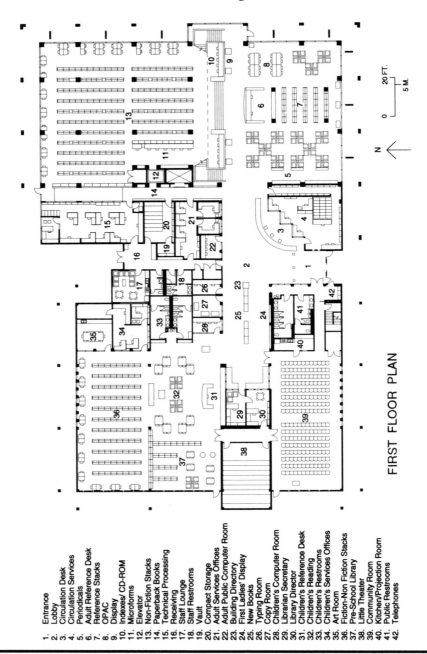

FIRST FLOOR PLAN

1. Entrance
2. Lobby
3. Circulation Desk
4. Circulation Services
5. Periodicals
6. Adult Reference Desk
7. Reference Stacks
8. OPAC
9. Display
10. Indexes/ CD-ROM
11. Microforms
12. Elevator
13. Non-Fiction Stacks
14. Paperback Books
15. Technical Processing
16. Receiving
17. Staff Lounge
18. Staff Restrooms
19. Vault
20. Compact Storage
21. Adult Services Offices
22. Adult Public Computer Room
23. Building Directory
24. First Ladies' Display
25. New Books
26. Typing Room
27. Copy Room
28. Children's Computer Room
29. Librarian Secretary
30. Library Director
31. Children's Reference Desk
32. Children's Reading
33. Children's Restrooms
34. Children's Services Offices
35. Art Room
36. Fiction-Non Fiction Stacks
37. Pre-School Library
38. Little Theater
39. Community Room
40. Kitchen/Projection Room
41. Public Restrooms
42. Telephones

Charles Walton Associates

Second Floor/Mezzanine Plan, Cerritos Public Library

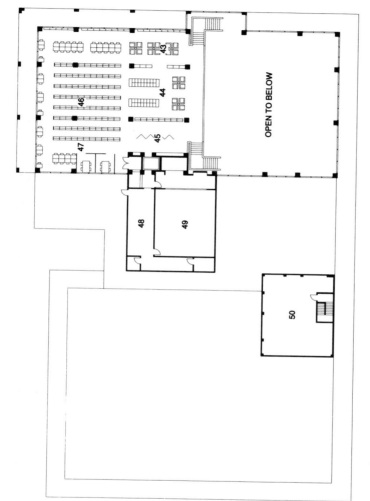

SECOND FLOOR / MEZZANINE PLAN

43. Young Adult Collection
44. Audiovisual Collection
45. Community Display
46. Fiction Stacks
47. Group Study
48. Storage
49. Mechanical Services
50. Mechanical Services

Charles Walton Associates

Petosky Public Library

Petosky, Michigan

Koster & Associates, Architects

Page 112: Existing Basement Plans: Proposed Rearrangement Basement Plans, Petosky Public Library

Page 113: Existing First Floor Plans: Proposed Rearrangement First Floor Plans, Petosky Public Library

Plans for the Petosky Public Library, Petosky, Michigan, were submitted by Koster & Associates, Architects (1220 West Sixth Street, Cleveland, Ohio 44113).

Existing Basement Plans: Proposed Rearrangement Basement Plans, Petosky Public Library

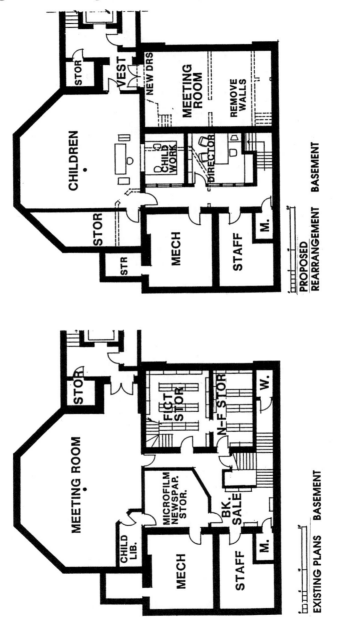

Koster & Associates, Architects

Existing First Floor Plans: Proposed Rearrangement First Floor Plans, Petosky Public Library

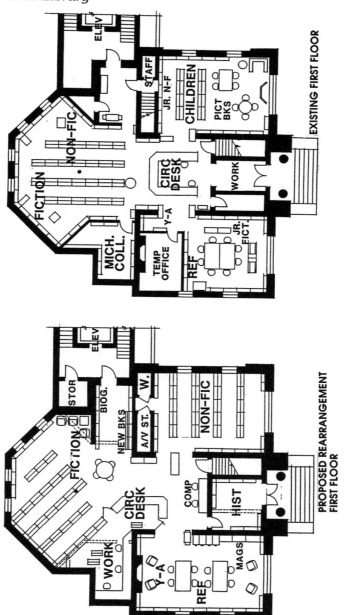

Koster & Associates, Architects

Norwalk Public Library

Norwalk, Ohio

Koster & Associates, Architects

Plans for the Norwalk Public Library, Norwalk, Ohio, were submitted by Koster & Associates, Architects (1220 West Sixth Street, Cleveland, Ohio 44113).

Existing Main Floor, Norwalk Public Library

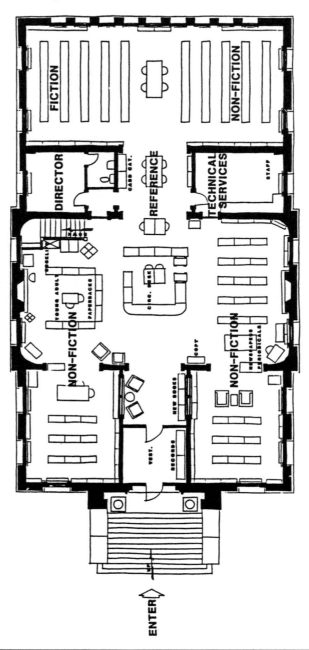

Koster & Associates, Architects

New Main Floor, Norwalk Public Library

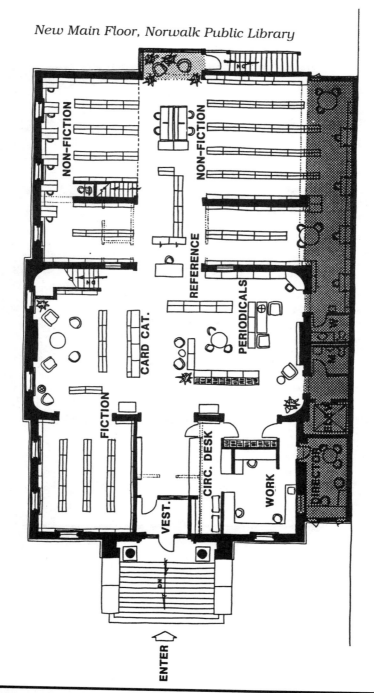

Koster & Associates, Architects

Existing Basement Floor, Norwalk Public Library

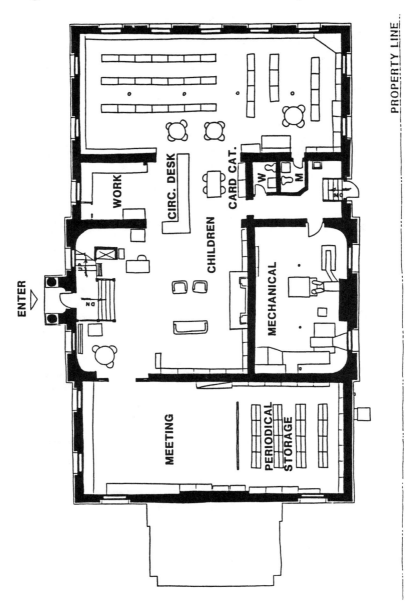

Koster & Associates, Architects

New Basement Floor, Norwalk Public Library

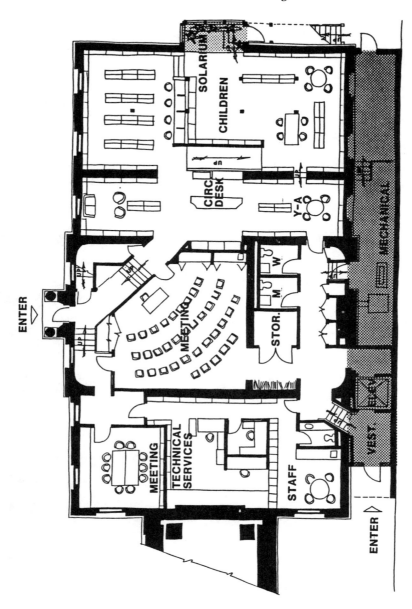

Koster & Associates, Architects

Carnegie West Branch Library
Cleveland, Ohio
Koster & Associates, Architects

Page 122: Existing First Floor Plan, Carnegie West Branch Library

Page 123: New First Floor Plan, Carnegie West Branch Library

Plans for the Carnegie West Branch Library in Cleveland, Ohio, were submitted by Koster & Associates, Architects (1220 West Sixth Street, Cleveland, Ohio 44113).

Existing First Floor Plan, Carnegie West Branch Library

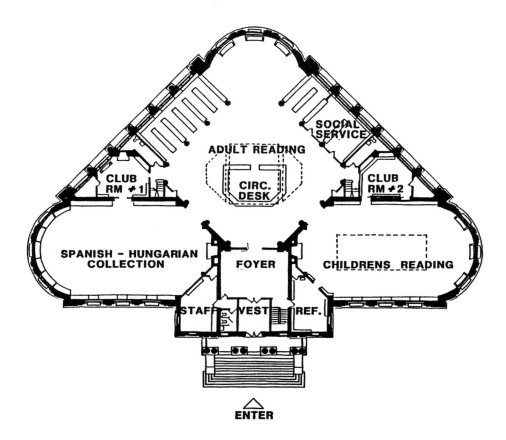

New First Floor Plan, Carnegie West Branch Library

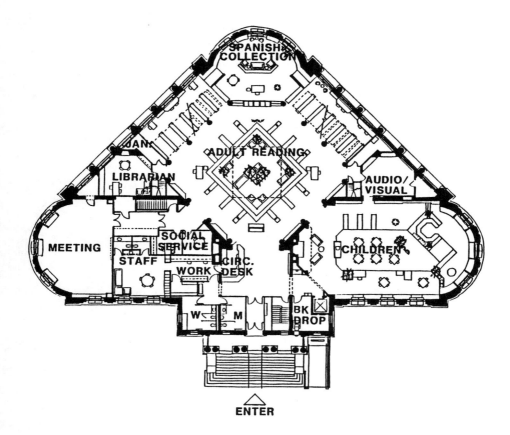

Peninsula Public Library

Peninsula, Ohio

Koster & Associates, Architects

Page 126: Existing Floor Plan, Peninsula Public Library

Page 127: New Floor Plan, Peninsula Public Library

Plans for the Peninsula Public Library, Peninsula, Ohio, were submitted by Koster & Associates, Architects (1220 West Sixth Street, Cleveland, Ohio 44113).

Existing Floor Plan, Peninsula Public Library

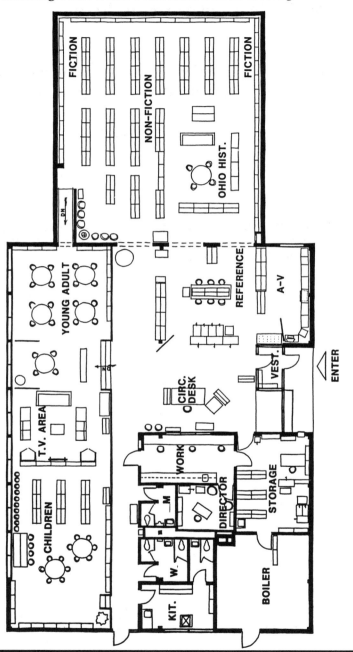

Koster & Associates, Architects

New Floor Plan, Peninsula Public Library

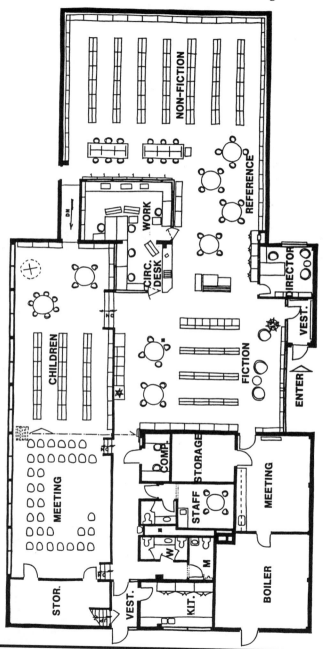

Koster & Associates, Architects

Bell Memorial Library

Mentone, Indiana

Koster & Associates, Architects

Page 130: Before Floor Plan, Bell Memorial Library

Page 131: After Floor Plan, Bell Memorial Library

Plans for the Bell Memorial Library, Mentone, Indiana, were submitted by Koster & Associates, Architects (1220 West Sixth Street, Cleveland, Ohio 44113).

Before Floor Plan, Bell Memorial Library

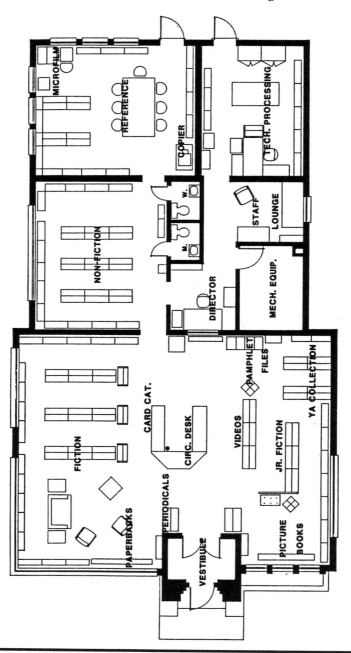

After Floor Plan, Bell Memorial Library

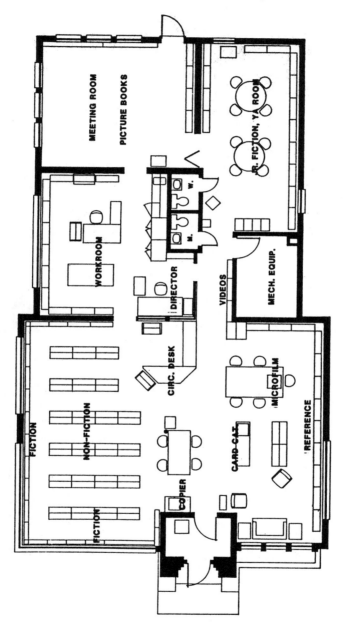

Koster & Associates, Architects

Clayton County Headquarters Library
Jonesboro, Georgia
Scogin Elam and Bray Architects, Inc.

Page 134: Left Half, Floor Plan, Clayton County Headquarters Library

Page 135: Right Half, Floor Plan, Clayton County Headquarters Library

Page 136: North and East Elevations, Clayton County Headquarters Library

The Clayton County Headquarters Library is a headquarters facility for a county-wide library system and a branch library located in Jonesboro, Georgia. It was completed in June 1988. The building area was 32,000 square feet and cost $2.1 million.

Scholars will not seek out obscure dissertation-supporting materials here; this library is designed to provide information for living life. A puppet show, a cooking class, a seed catalog ... a welcoming, friendly place that says come in and browse awhile.

Credits for Clayton County Library System Headquarters and Main Branch: Merrill Elam and Mack Scogin, Scogin Elam and Bray Architects, Inc.; with Lloyd Bray, Project Director; and Rick Sellers, Isabelle Millet, Tom Crosby, David Murphree, Dick Spangler, and Ennis Parker.

Clayton County Headquarters Library won the National AIA/ALA Award for Excellence, 1991; the AIA National Honor Award, 1989; and the South Atlantic Region Conference AIA Honor Award, 1988.

Left Half, Floor Plan, Clayton County Headquarters Library

Key
 1—Study
 2—Main reading
 3—Office
 4—Board Room
 5—Computer
 6—Director
 7—Circulation
 8—Genealogy
 9—Future Porch
10—Children's area
11—Lecture
12—Entry
13—Staff Lounge

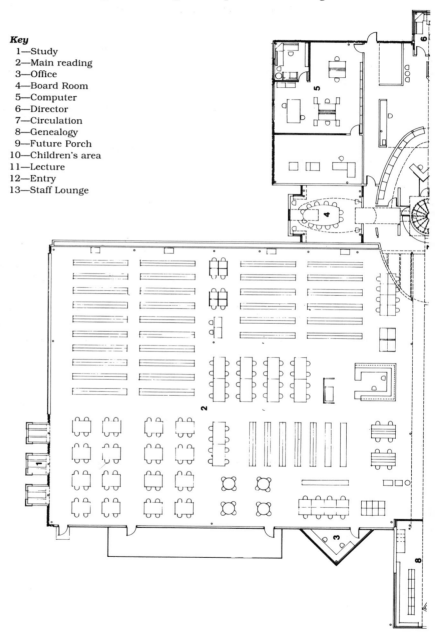

Scogin Elam and Bray Architects, Inc.

Right Half, Floor Plan, Clayton County Headquarters Library

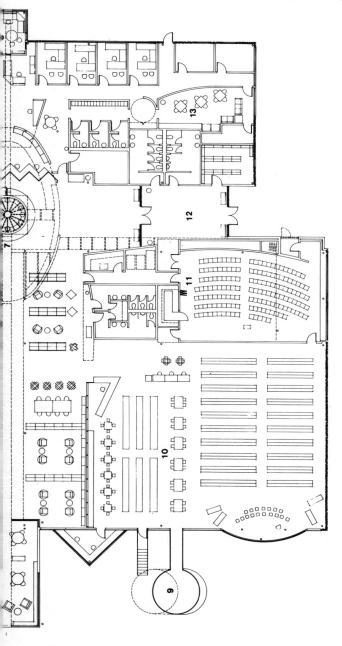

Scogin Elam and Bray Architects, Inc.

North and East Elevations, Clayton County Headquarters Library

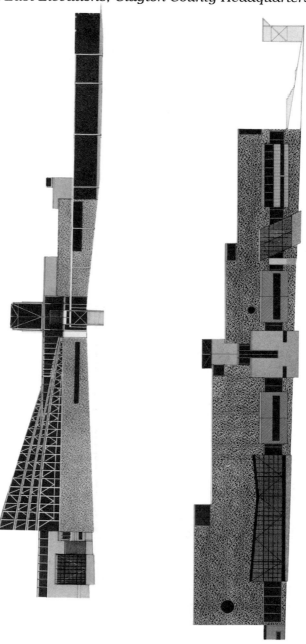

Scogin Elam and Bray Architects, Inc.

Buckhead Branch Library
Atlanta, Georgia
Scogin Elam and Bray Architects, Inc.

The new Buckhead Branch Library in Atlanta, Georgia, is atop a crest that commands a spectacular view of downtown Atlanta. The need for the new library emanated from the inability of the old facility (located on the same site) to meet the higher-technology demands of its patrons. The new library was completed in winter 1989; approximately 20,000 square feet were added to the existing building at a cost of $1.6 million.

Credits for Buckhead Branch Library: Scogin Elam and Bray Architects, Inc. Mark Scogin, Merrill Elam, and Lloyd Bray, with Susan Desko, Jeff Atwood, John Lauer, Ellen Hooker, Patricia Kerlin, Ron Mitchell, Isabelle Millet, Criss Mills, Carlos Tardio, Roy Farley, and Sean McLendon.

The Buckhead Branch Library won the National AIA Award for Excellence, 1993; the National AIA/ALA Award for Excellence, 1991; the Georgia AIA Award for Excellence in Architecture, 1990; and the Urban Design Commission Award of Excellence, 1990.

Left Half Floor Plan, Buckhead Branch Library

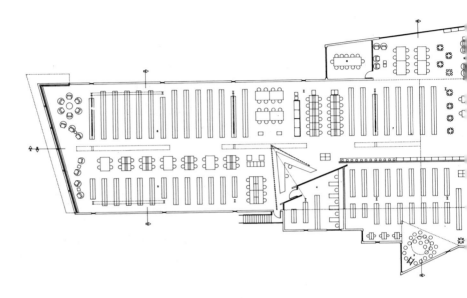

Right Half Floor Plan, Buckhead Branch Library

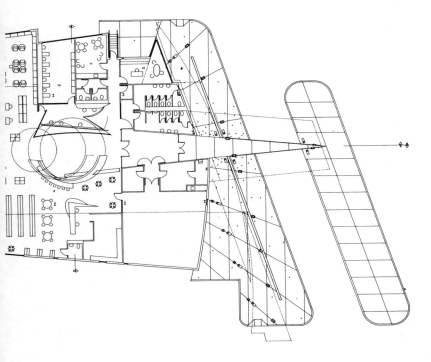

Scogin Elam and Bray Architects, Inc.

Elevations, Buckhead Branch Library

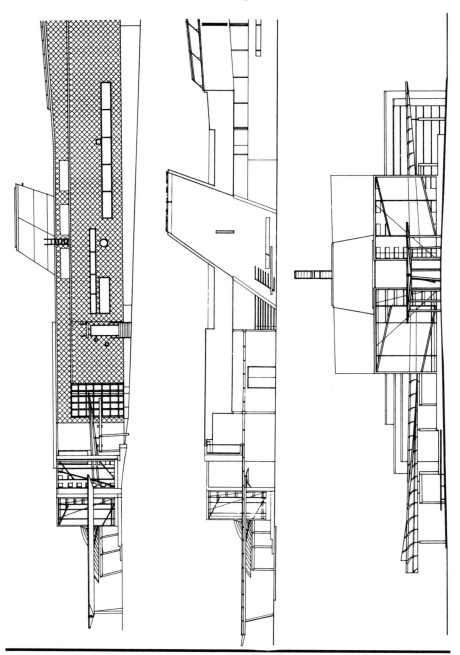

Scogin Elam and Bray Architects, Inc.

3-D View, Buckhead Branch Library

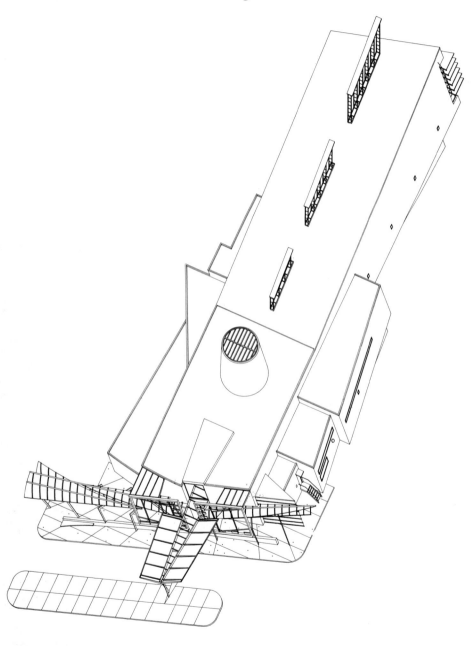

Scogin Elam and Bray Architects, Inc.

Carroll County District Library

Carrollton, Ohio

Beck and Tabeling, Architects, Inc.

Page 144: Remodeled Floor Plan, Carroll County District Library

Plan for the remodeled Carroll County District Library was submitted by Beck and Tabeling, Architects, Inc. (3689 IRA Road, P.O. Box 1244, Bath, Ohio 44210-1244).

Remodeled Floor Plan, Carroll County District Library

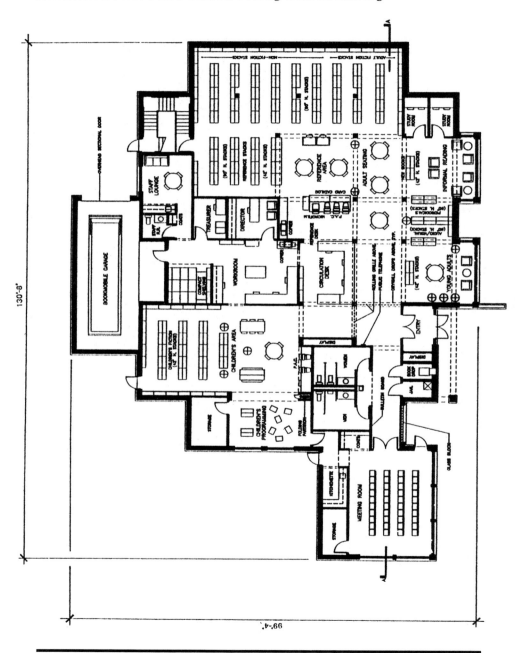

Beck and Tabeling, Architects, Inc.

Champaign County Library

Urbana, Illinois

Beck and Tabeling, Architects, Inc.

Page 146: Remodeled Floor Plan, Champaign County Library

Plan for the remodeled Champaign County Library was submitted by Beck and Tabeling, Architects, Inc. (3689 IRA Road, P.O. Box 1244, Bath, Ohio 44210-1244).

Remodeled Floor Plan, Champaign County Library

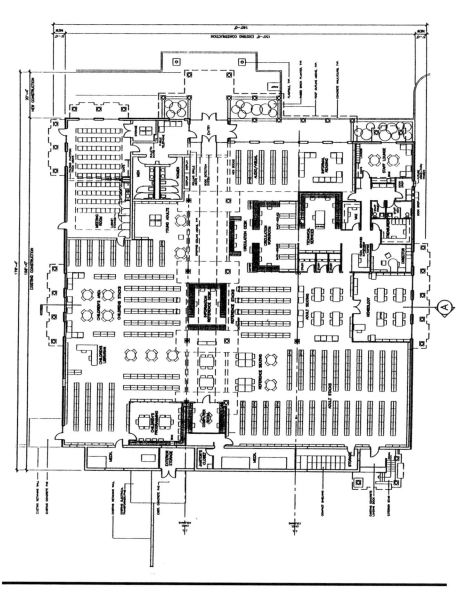

Beck and Tabeling, Architects, Inc.

Index